"Danielle's recipes consistently impress and *Make It Easy* checks off all the right boxes: it is accessible, inventive, and straightforward enough for anyone to follow. I'm excited to add this beautiful cookbook to my collection!"

—Gina Homolka, creator of Skinnytaste and author of the Skinnytaste cookbooks

"*Make It Easy* is a game-changer for anyone looking to simplify their kitchen routine. Recipes like Beef and Zucchini Enchiladas Verdes and Sheet-Pan Smashed-Potato Nachos are just a taste of the healthy, stress-free take-out alternatives Danielle offers for busy nights. Trust me, Danielle's got the secret sauce to making quick eats that are packed with flavor and goodness."

—Jocelyn Delk Adams, author of *Everyday Grand: Soulful Recipes for Celebrating Life's Big and Small Moments*

MAKE IT
EASY

DANIELLE WALKER

MAKE IT
EASY

A Healthy Meal Prep
& Menu Planning Guide

Photographs by Erin Scott

TEN SPEED PRESS
California | New York

Contents

Introduction

Are you tired of scrambling to make dinner at the last minute (and resorting to unhealthy takeout or frozen dinners)? Does the thought of planning, shopping for, and making five to seven dinners a week stress you out? Well, here's some good news: By dedicating just a couple of hours each week to meal prepping and menu planning, you can have a variety of nutritious, homemade meals readily available without spending hours in the kitchen.

In this cookbook, I will help you transform your eating habits, save time, and reduce waste—while enjoying incredibly delicious and satisfying meals that also happen to be free from grains, gluten, and lactose. Did you know that the average American family of four throws out between $1,600 and $1,800 a year in produce alone? In the US, we waste more than $408 billion in food annually, and a lot of that waste can be attributed to poor planning and impulse buying.

If you've long wanted to become a better menu planner and an advance meal prepper, I'm here to guide you through the process step-by-step. I'll provide easy-to-follow instructions, helpful tips, and foolproof recipes that have gotten the stamp of approval from gluten-free and paleo eaters, as well as from those who can eat whatever they want. I've served these recipes to kids and adults alike, and while everyone's palate and preferences are different, I am confident that everyone you cook these for will love them. (And they'll be asking you for the recipes and meal plans, too.)

My goal with this book is to eliminate the stress you feel about what to eat, and teach you how to plan meals that use a variety of ingredients to their full potential. Using the menu plans in this book and my tips on what to prepare ahead of time will allow you to spend less time in the kitchen every day, while providing yourself and those around your table with nourishing meals.

To begin, first read through the next few sections of the book to understand how and why the recipes are laid out the way they are, to discover some secrets for very quick meals (hello, newly stocked freezer and ready-to-go pantry), and to learn more about the methods that will make you a meal planning superstar.

When it comes to the fifteen meticulously crafted meal plans and recipes, you don't have to start with Week 1, but if the recipes in that chapter speak to you, then jump right in! You can use the weekly meal plans in any order you like. Some of the plans utilize frozen, make-ahead meals or components that were prepared in previous weeks, but I've also explained how you can improvise if you end up skipping around the book.

Each weekly meal plan comes with an accompanying shopping list, along with a QR code to scan so you can take a digital copy with you to the grocery store. After scanning, you will find an option to access the weekly meal plan shopping lists by recipe, too, in case you only want to cook three of the meals that week or you need to double a recipe.

These meal plans and recipes are intentionally designed to reduce waste, be sustainable, and use all the ingredients in your fridge. Say goodbye to spoiled bunches of herbs and forgotten jars of condiments hidden behind bottles on your fridge door, and hello to a pantry, freezer, and fridge stocked with tasty meals. By following these meal plans, you'll not only minimize waste but also take the guesswork out of menu planning. Shopping will be a breeze, as you confidently pick up the items you need, knowing they'll be used in delicious, healthy meals throughout the week.

I've designed these recipes to be family-friendly and cater to different flavor preferences and dietary needs. Whether you have picky eaters to feed or have your own special dietary requirements, you'll find recipes to satisfy everyone at your table. And I'll walk you through prepping ahead or even making whole components or dishes in advance. That means you can spend less time in the kitchen during the week and more time enjoying meals with your loved ones.

Get ready to experience the convenience, health benefits, and, honestly, the joy and satisfaction of meal prepping and menu planning. With this book as your guide, you'll be an expert in make-ahead and quick-to-the-table dinners in no time, giving you the kitchen confidence you've been seeking, the nourishment your body craves, and a repertoire of go-to meals your family returns to again and again.

Danielle

Hi, and thank you so much for picking up this book! I'm Danielle, and I've authored six other books containing grain-free, paleo, and gluten-free meals:

Against All Grain: Delectable Paleo Recipes to Eat Well and Feel Great

Danielle Walker's Against All Grain Meals Made Simple: Gluten-Free, Dairy-Free, and Paleo Recipes to Make Anytime

Danielle Walker's Against All Grain Celebrations: A Year of Gluten-Free, Dairy-Free, and Paleo Recipes for Every Occasion

Danielle Walker's Eat What You Love: Everyday Comfort Food You Crave

Food Saved Me: My Journey of Finding Health and Hope through the Power of Food

Danielle Walker's Healthy in a Hurry: Real Life. Real Food. Real Fast.

Find me at daniellewalker.com and join me over on social media for videos, tutorials, and daily life:

Instagram.com/daniellewalker

Facebook.com/againstallgrain

Youtube.com/againstallgrain

Pinterest.com/daniellewalker

Once you've cooked your way through the book or if you're feeling inspired and creative, be sure to download my free app, Shop the Book (shopthebook .com). It allows you to craft your own weekly menu plans and create shopping lists using the recipes in this book—and from all five of my other cookbooks!—with just the touch of a button. If you choose to make the meal plans as designed in this book, you can also add all of the ingredients to your digital shopping lists and take your device with you to the store instead of this heavy book.

Part 1
Getting Started

Meal-Prepping Personas: Which Type Are You?

The traditional meal-prepping approach of cooking all the main components of multiple meals during one designated prep day might not be feasible for everyone, especially if you have a busy schedule or a large family. That's why I've taken multiple circumstances into account and organized this book a little differently from most. Instead of one-size-fits-all meal prepping, I've divided the chapters into full weekly meal plans and included copious notes and tips at the bottom of each recipe that take different types of meal prepping into account—because, hey, our needs change depending on the time of year, the age of our kids, the size of our family, or the levels of stress that come with work, life, and parenting.

If you have some extra time in your life (that's wishful thinking for me, but a woman can dream!) and love to be ultra-organized, perhaps you are a Component Prepper, who preps ahead to create dump-and-stir meals during the week. You set aside a day at the beginning of the week to cook a variety of proteins, vegetables, and starches that can be used in different meals all week. This way, you have the flexibility to mix and match these prepared components into quick and delicious lunches or improvised dinners.

On the other hand, if you find yourself caught up in work, sports, or school activities, you might be a Semi-Homemade Prepper, who relies on the recipe tips that help you shave off time in the kitchen. This means relying on store-bought shortcuts like jarred sauces, precut vegetables, premade meatballs, or a rotisserie chicken, alleviating the pressure to make every single component from scratch.

Following are the six meal-prepper personas I have identified among myself, my friends, and my readers. Chances are, you can relate to at least one of these approaches, if not a few of them, depending on what your life looks like today. But even if you don't see yourself here or feel like you change your persona from week to week (I do!), the meal prepping and menu planning methods in this book will work for you, I promise.

THE COMPONENT PREPPER

This person focuses on preparing individual components of meals in advance. They take the time to perform tasks like browning a large amount of ground beef or roasting multiple chickens at once. By doing so, they have ready-to-go ingredients that can be used in various dishes throughout the week. The Component Prepper also complements their components with precut vegetables and premade or jarred sauces, enabling them to quickly assemble meals when needed.

If you are a Component Prepper, you'll like these recipes:

THE BATCH COOKER

This person takes the concept of meal prepping to the next level by cooking large quantities of food and freezing it in individual portions or full meals to reheat later. This approach provides ready-made meals for those days when time is scarce or a quick solution is needed. The Batch Cooker might often be cooking for only one or two people because, by cooking in bulk and freezing portions, they can efficiently manage their meals and easily defrost and reheat them as needed.

If you are a Batch Cooker, you'll like these recipes:

THE SEMI-HOMEMADE PREPPER

This person prefers simplicity and convenience, relying on store-bought meal-prep options. They focus on meals with ten ingredients or fewer, swap store-bought sauces for homemade, pull apart a rotisserie chicken rather than roasting their own, and purchase precut vegetables to minimize time spent in the kitchen. By utilizing already prepared ingredients from the store, the Semi-Homemade Prepper enjoys delicious and nutritious meals without extensive cooking or preparation.

If you are a Semi-Homemade Prepper, you'll like these recipes:

THE FREEZER PREPPER

This person follows a strategy of cooking meals in advance and freezing them for later consumption. Like the Batch Cooker, they cook meals in larger quantities but with the intention of eating some of them at a later time. This method is particularly useful for individuals who have busy schedules or want to have a variety of meals readily available. This allows them to save time and effort during busy periods while still enjoying home-cooked meals. The Freezer Prepper often creates two meals at once, a method I describe as a freezer kit in this book (see also pages 17–23). The recipes are simple enough to not require precise measurements and can be divided into two meals—one to cook now, and one to store in the freezer for later.

If you are a Freezer Prepper, you'll like these recipes:

THE PANTRY PREPPER

This person does not engage in meal prepping. They rely on their pantry and food supplies in their freezer to create meals spontaneously without any preplanning or preparation. This approach may not work for every meal, but the Pantry Prepper really knows how to forage through their kitchen and use up the ingredients they have.

If you are a Pantry Prepper, you'll like these recipes:

Magic Meatball Pasta 189

Creamy Dill–Sardine Salad with Capers 232

Coconut–Pumpkin Curry 233

Mediterranean Salmon Salad 234

Tomato Soup and Grilled Prosciutto-and-Pear Cheese Sandwiches 235

Tuna Casserole 236

Breakfast-for-Dinner: Sheet-Pan Pancakes and Bacon 237

Tuna Salad with Apples and Pumpkin Seeds 238

Lemony Shrimp Pasta with Artichokes 239

Sausage Skillets, Four Ways 240

Spiced Sweet Potato Soup 244

Baked Pesto Gnocchi and Sausage 245

THE MORPH-MEAL COOK

This person leans on their creativity and resourcefulness when it comes to cooking. They excel at repurposing leftovers into new and distinct dishes and may intentionally make extra portions for just this purpose. By transforming cooked ingredients, the Morph-Meal Cook minimizes food waste and adds variety to their meals. This approach is perfect for those who enjoy experimenting in the kitchen and optimizing their resources.

If you are a Morph-Meal Cook, you'll like how these recipes can be repurposed:

Make Granny's Spaghetti with Meat Sauce (page 144) and use it in Cheats Minestrone (page 146) and Italian Cottage Pie (page 149)

Make Chicken Tinga (page 206) and use it in Taco Skillet Hash (page 210)

Make Shredded Beef (page 156) and use it in Beef and Zucchini Enchiladas Verdes (page 163), and Steak and Eggs Breakfast Tacos (page 164)

Make Shredded Carnitas Pork (page 104) and use it in Fried Pineapple and Pork Rice (page 107) and Cuban Pork Sheet-Pan Quesadillas (page 108)

Make Cheesy Nacho Sauce (page 218) and use it in Tex-Mex Mac and Cheese (page 224) and Sheet-Pan Smashed-Potato Nachos (page 222)

How to Navigate This Book

Menu planning and meal prepping are game changers for busy individuals seeking a balanced lifestyle; they save time, reduce food waste, and help you to maintain a healthy lifestyle. However, when you eat a grain-free, gluten-free, paleo diet, there's still a lot of prep involved—and that takes planning. To make the process easily achievable, I've already done the planning for you. Each of the fifteen weeks of meal plans (see page 39) include the following components:

Recipes: There are four recipes and an accompanying grocery list for each weekly menu. I have also recommended one back-pocket dinner (a meal built from ingredients you already have in your pantry or freezer; see page 24) that would pair well with that week's other meals. If you have stocked your pantry and freezer well (see page 24), this fifth meal shouldn't require any additional groceries. Skip around the book and choose menu plans that suit your preferences or work chronologically through them all. Except for the seafood dishes (which should be prepared as suggested for maximum freshness), you can decide for yourself when to cook each recipe during the week.

If you do work chronologically through all fifteen menu plans, you will have a treasure in your freezer at the end: two weeks of meal plans made up exclusively of freezer recipes you have stashed away. It's like having a personal chef for two weeks! Just scan the QR code at left to download the freezer meal plans.

In addition to the weeknight dinners within the weekly meal plans, I've given you even more recipes in Make-Ahead Breakfasts (page 249), Make-Ahead Snacks (page 259), Make-Ahead Sides (page 267), and Make-Ahead Desserts (page 275) to start and end your days with ease.

Grocery Lists: These are your shopping lists for each week's four recipes. I've organized the items based on grocery store departments. I set apart the Cupboard & Counter list, most of which you should already have on hand if you have a well-stocked pantry (see page 24). I did not include ingredients in the grocery lists for that week's recommended back-pocket dinner, since you probably already have those items stocked or may choose to take that night off. Scan the QR code next to each list to access the ingredients organized by recipe in case you want to omit a recipe one week or need to make a substitute.

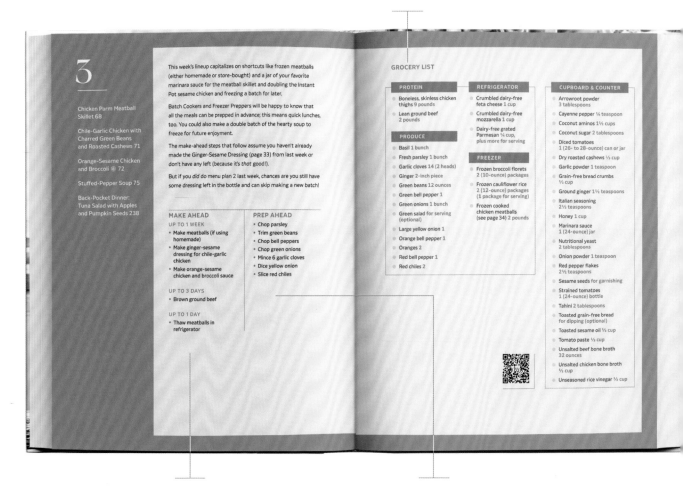

3

Chicken Parm Meatball
Skillet 68

Chile-Garlic Chicken with
Charred Green Beans
and Roasted Cashews 71

Orange-Sesame Chicken
and Broccoli ⓦ 72

Stuffed-Pepper Soup 75

Back-Pocket Dinner:
Tuna Salad with Apples
and Pumpkin Seeds 238

This week's lineup capitalizes on shortcuts like frozen meatballs (either homemade or store-bought) and a jar of your favorite marinara sauce for the meatball skillet and doubling the Instant Pot sesame chicken and freezing a batch for later.

Batch Cookers and Freezer Preppers will be happy to know that all the meals can be prepped in advance; this means quick lunches, too. You could also make a double batch of the hearty soup to freeze for future enjoyment.

The make-ahead steps that follow assume you haven't already made the Ginger-Sesame Dressing (page 33) from last week or don't have any left (because it's *that* good!).

But if you *did* do menu plan 2 last week, chances are you still have some dressing left in the bottle and can skip making a new batch!

MAKE AHEAD

UP TO 1 WEEK
- Make meatballs (if using homemade)
- Make ginger-sesame dressing for chile-garlic chicken
- Make orange-sesame chicken and broccoli sauce

UP TO 3 DAYS
- Brown ground beef

UP TO 1 DAY
- Thaw meatballs in refrigerator

PREP AHEAD
- Chop parsley
- Trim green beans
- Chop bell peppers
- Chop green onions
- Mince 6 garlic cloves
- Dice yellow onion
- Slice red chiles

GROCERY LIST

PROTEIN
- Boneless, skinless chicken thighs 9 pounds
- Lean ground beef 2 pounds

PRODUCE
- Basil 1 bunch
- Fresh parsley 1 bunch
- Garlic cloves 14 (2 heads)
- Ginger 2-inch piece
- Green beans 12 ounces
- Green bell pepper 1
- Green onions 1 bunch
- Green salad for serving (optional)
- Large yellow onion 1
- Orange bell pepper 1
- Oranges 2
- Red bell pepper 1
- Red chiles 2

REFRIGERATOR
- Crumbled dairy-free feta cheese 1 cup
- Crumbled dairy-free mozzarella 1 cup
- Dairy-free grated Parmesan ¼ cup, plus more for serving

FREEZER
- Frozen broccoli florets 2 (10-ounce) packages
- Frozen cauliflower rice 2 (12-ounce) packages (1 package for serving)
- Frozen cooked chicken meatballs (see page 34) 2 pounds

CUPBOARD & COUNTER
- Arrowroot powder 3 tablespoons
- Cayenne pepper ¼ teaspoon
- Coconut aminos 1½ cups
- Coconut sugar 2 tablespoons
- Diced tomatoes 1 (26- to 28-ounce) can or jar
- Dry roasted cashews ½ cup
- Garlic powder 1 teaspoon
- Grain-free bread crumbs ½ cup
- Ground ginger 1½ teaspoons
- Italian seasoning 2½ teaspoons
- Honey 1 cup
- Marinara sauce 1 (24-ounce) jar
- Nutritional yeast 2 tablespoons
- Onion powder 1 teaspoon
- Red pepper flakes 2½ teaspoons
- Sesame seeds for garnishing
- Strained tomatoes 1 (24-ounce) bottle
- Tahini 2 tablespoons
- Toasted grain-free bread for dipping (optional)
- Toasted sesame oil ½ cup
- Tomato paste ½ cup
- Unsalted beef bone broth 32 ounces
- Unsalted chicken bone broth ½ cup
- Unseasoned rice vinegar ½ cup

Make-Ahead Steps: These lists identify the parts of the recipes you can make in advance (along with storage information) for the entire week—if you are having a rock star week and have time to designate a full prep day. Sometimes the complete entree can be made ahead, and other times components, such as a marinade or dressing, can be premade to save time. These lists are also broken down by individual recipe on the recipe page.

Prep-Ahead Steps: These lists identify the tasks you can complete ahead of time for the entire week, such as chopping vegetables or marinating meat. If you prefer to prep each night just before you cook, these same steps are broken down by individual recipe on the recipe page.

Active Time: Listed at the top of each recipe, this refers to the amount of time you will be actively engaged in preparing and cooking the dish. It does not include passive time, such as marinating or waiting for something to slow-cook, for example. Where there are multiple cooking methods listed, the active time was computed using the first one, as it is my preferred method. Every cook preps at a different pace, so these are only rough estimates, but they'll give you a good sense of how long it takes to get a dish on the table.

5

Enchilada-Stuffed Sweet Potatoes

SERVES 6
ACTIVE TIME: 55 MINUTES

PREP AHEAD

Scrub and cook sweet potatoes

Dice onion and poblano peppers

MAKE AHEAD

Refrigerate enchilada sauce up to 1 month; freeze up to 6 months

Refrigerate cooked sweet potatoes and filling up to 5 days

Freeze filling up to 4 months

NOTES AND SHORTCUTS

Enchilada sauce brands: Siete and Sprouts

Use any grain-free taco seasoning; check for rice starch or other anti-caking agents

To cook sweet potatoes in an Instant Pot: Pour 1 cup water into cooker, add a steamer insert, and place sweet potatoes on insert. Secure lid, set valve to seal. Cook on high pressure with a 15-minute timer. Quick-release pressure.

Sub leftover shredded beef (see page 156) or shredded rotisserie chicken for ground meat

6 medium sweet potatoes, scrubbed clean

1 tablespoon avocado oil

1 teaspoon coarse sea salt

FILLING

2 tablespoons avocado oil

1 yellow onion, diced

2 medium poblano chiles, seeds removed and diced

4 garlic cloves, minced

1½ teaspoons sea salt

2 pounds ground meat (chicken, bison, beef, or turkey)

RED ENCHILADA SAUCE

3 tablespoons ghee

3 tablespoons arrowroot powder

3½ tablespoons Healthy in a Hurry Taco Seasoning (page 37)

7 ounces tomato paste

2 cups unsalted chicken bone broth

Dairy-free sour cream, sliced avocado, cilantro, sliced black olives, and shredded lettuce for topping (optional)

Preheat oven to 400°F. Line a baking sheet with parchment paper or aluminum foil.

Rub skins of sweet potatoes all over with oil and pat with coarse salt. Using a fork, prick skins a few times and place on prepared baking sheet. Bake until tender, about 40 minutes.

To make filling: While potatoes are baking, in a large skillet over medium-high heat, warm oil until it shimmers. Add onion, poblanos, garlic, and sea salt and sauté for 5 minutes. Add ground meat and continue cooking until meat is cooked through and vegetables are softened, about 10 minutes.

To make sauce: While filling is cooking, in a medium saucepan over medium heat, melt ghee. Whisk in arrowroot powder and cook for 2 minutes. Add taco seasoning and stir for 2 minutes longer, until fragrant. Add tomato paste and broth and whisk until smooth. Turn heat to low and let simmer for 5 minutes to thicken. (Let cool completely before storing.)

Cut slits in tops of cooked sweet potatoes and open them up a bit. Spoon ⅓ cup filling into each and top with 2 to 3 tablespoons sauce.

Serve with sour cream, avocado, cilantro, olives, and lettuce, if desired.

96   MAKE IT EASY

Notes and Shortcuts: Provided with every recipe, these are my tips for saving time, finding the best-quality ingredients, or making substitutions to meet your dietary needs or utilize what you have on hand.

Shop the Book App: Once again, you can download my free cookbook companion app to make planning your own custom menu plans and shopping lists automated and effortless. The app can also create grocery lists for recipes that aren't part of the weekly menu plan, such as Back-Pocket Dinners, Make-Ahead Breakfasts, and Make-Ahead Snacks.

PREP DAY GUIDE

The following are general guidelines for storing the prepped components of your meals but review the recipe-specific notes in each meal plan as well.

INGREDIENT	STORAGE
Avocados (halved)	Store with half an onion to prevent browning. Place the avocado halves, with pit intact, in an airtight container with the cut-side facing up. Separate the avocado halves from the onion with a small piece of plastic wrap or a damp paper towel. Seal the container tightly and store in the refrigerator up to 3 days.
Bell peppers (sliced)	Store in an airtight container in the refrigerator up to 5 days.
Celery and carrots (raw, chopped)	Store submerged in filtered water in an airtight container in the refrigerator up to 7 days. Drain and add fresh water every few days if water becomes cloudy.
Chicken (cooked and shredded)	Store in an airtight container in the refrigerator up to 5 days.
Eggs (hard-boiled)	Store unpeeled in an airtight container in the refrigerator up to 7 days.
Fruit (cut or sliced)	Store in an airtight container or a resealable plastic bag in the refrigerator up to 5 days.
Herbs (fresh)	Trim the stems and place herbs in a jar with filtered water. Loosely cover the jar with a plastic bag and store in the refrigerator up to 7 days.
Leafy greens (spinach, lettuce, kale)	Wash, dry, and store in an airtight container (or a resealable plastic bag with a paper towel to absorb excess moisture) in the refrigerator up to 5 days.
Marinades or marinating meats	Place meat in a resealable plastic bag or a shallow, nonreactive container (glass or stainless steel). Cover meat with marinade, ensuring it is fully submerged. Seal or cover the container and refrigerate. Marinating times will vary depending on the meat and the recipe but generally marinate in the refrigerator:
Poultry	2 to 24 hours
Beef	4 to 24 hours
Pork	2 to 12 hours
Seafood	15 minutes to 2 hours
Onion and garlic (diced)	Store in an airtight container in the refrigerator up to 7 days.
Sauces and dressings	Store in airtight mason jars, with pour spout lids for easy usage, in the refrigerator 10 to 14 days.
Vegetables (roasted)	Store in an airtight container in the refrigerator for up to 5 days.

Freeze It: Your Secret Weapon for Stress-Free Meals

Whenever I'm preparing a meal, I think about my future self. Will there be a busy day next week or next month when I would greatly appreciate finding a fully made dinner in the freezer, ready to be reheated or quickly cooked in the Instant Pot? The answer is always a resounding yes. Regardless of the size of your freezer, from a spacious garage unit to an extremely compact dorm-sized one, or the freezer attached to your refrigerator, having a few go-to meals, sauces, and breakfast options stored away never fails to save you time and alleviate stress.

Dedicating a few hours on a weekend or on a specific day to prep and freeze multiple meals can save you so much time. You can even just double a meal you're already making. That means more time for other activities or to simply relax after a long day.

Using the freezer for meal prepping can also be budget friendly. Buying ingredients in bulk and taking advantage of seasonal produce can help you save money, too. Freezing leftovers and excess portions helps you to stretch your budget and avoid wasting food. If you're cooking for one or two, make the meals in this book and store half in the freezer for another full week of meals in the future. Or freeze them as individual portions to take to work for lunch or while you're on the run for car pool.

FREEZER ICONS ❄

While freezing tips are given for nearly all the recipes in the book, the recipes marked with the above icon, as well as those listed with the Freezer Prepper (page 8), were intentionally created to be prepped in batches for the freezer.

MAKE THE MOST OF YOUR FREEZER

Choose the right containers: Use freezer-safe containers or bags with a tight seal to prevent air from entering. I have a drawerful of Stasher-brand bags (the Stand-Up Mega Bag works great for meals), glass containers with sealed lids (OXO and Ello are my favorites), and recycled ghee jars. Opt for clear containers or freezer bags to easily see the contents without opening each container.

Prep the food: Properly prepare the food before freezing, including washing fruits and vegetables, blanching vegetables, and trimming excess fat from meats. Cut items into smaller portions if needed.

Freeze without ingredients to save space: When preparing recipes for freezing, omit large-volume ingredients, such as wine or broth, to save space in your freezer. Instead, include a note on the bag or container indicating the missing ingredients and their quantities for quick reference when you're ready to cook. Whether you plan to use a slow cooker or an Instant Pot, having a clear reminder of the additional ingredients needed will make the cooking process more efficient without having to look up the recipe.

Package and label the containers: Place the food in the chosen containers, leaving some headspace to allow for expansion. Label the containers using painter's tape and a marker for easy identification. Date each container for easy tracking and to ensure timely usage.

Cool ingredients before freezing: Allow hot or cooked foods to cool down completely, ideally in the refrigerator, before placing them in the freezer.

Freeze quickly: Freeze foods as quickly as possible to maintain food quality and prevent bacteria growth. Freeze larger items in individual or meal-sized portions to reduce waste. Consider using recycled ghee jars or silicone muffin molds for sauces, dressings, broths, soups, and more.

Pack your freezer strategically: Divide your freezer into different sections based on food categories. Use clear bins or designated areas for meats, vegetables, fruits, dairy, and so on. Keep similar items together to find them easily and avoid overcrowding.

Maintain an inventory list: Keep a written or digital inventory of the items in your freezer and fridge. Include details, such as the name, quantity, and storage date. Update the list as you add or remove items. I use a magnetic white board stuck directly to my fridge and freezer to list meal-prepped foods, fully prepared meals, and lists of sauces or miscellaneous items at a glance. Alternatively, use a shared Google document for a digital approach to tracking your freezer inventory.

Use the First In, First Out (FIFO) method: Arrange items based on the FIFO principle, using the oldest items first to ensure freshness and prevent food from being forgotten.

DEFROST SAFELY AND MAINTAIN FLAVOR

When it comes time to defrost your meals, you can use a few different methods:

In the fridge: For the best results, thaw frozen meals, components, or raw meats in the refrigerator. Place the item on a plate or in a container to catch any liquid that accumulates. Allow enough time for the food to thaw completely; for large items and full meals, that may require 24 hours or more.

In cold water: To thaw food more quickly than in the fridge, place the frozen food in a sealed bag and submerge it in a bowl of cold water. Change the water every 30 minutes to ensure a safe and efficient thaw.

In the microwave: While this is my least-favorite method, most microwaves have a defrost function that can thaw frozen foods based on weight or type. But be careful if you use this method because some microwaves will partially cook the food during the defrosting process.

See the next chapter to learn about the best methods for reheating your now-thawed meals as well as leftovers.

HOW TO MAKE FREEZER PUCKS

I put my silicone muffin molds to use in my kitchen for much more than baking a batch of Blueberry Muffins (page 250). Whether I'm freezing sauces, soups, broths, dressings, or even cake batters (page 281), making individually frozen "pucks" is the ultimate space-saving solution and easiest way to defrost only what you need quickly.

My set of jumbo molds holds approximately 1 cup of liquid per mold, and my regular molds each hold ⅓ cup. When I need 1 cup of broth for a recipe, I know I can pull out three standard pucks or one jumbo puck. Similarly, if a recipe calls for 2 cups of my Cheesy Nacho Sauce (page 218), I can pull out six standard pucks or two jumbo pucks. The pucks defrost super quickly compared to a large frozen portion and make a perfect single serving of soup.

To turn the following ingredients into freezer pucks:

Avocado: Freeze mashed avocado that is about to go bad up to 3 months; defrost for easy avocado toast or guacamole

Bone broth and soup: Cool completely, then freeze up to 4 to 6 months

Canned coconut milk: Freeze up to 3 months; use frozen in smoothies or defrost for recipes

Cheesy Nacho Sauce (page 218): Cool completely, then freeze up to 6 months

Dairy-free yogurt: Freeze up to 3 months; use frozen in smoothies or defrost for recipes

Herbs: Chop leftover herbs and cover in olive oil; freeze up to 6 months

Mug Cake Batter (page 281): Freeze up to 6 months

Sauces: Cool completely sauces like Granny's Meat Sauce (page 144); Dairy-Free Ranch Dressing (page 32), Dairy-Free Pesto (page 32), and Green Goddess Dressing (page 33) can be stored immediately, freeze 3 to 4 months

From Cold to Gold:
How to Reheat Everything

Intentionally creating leftovers, or preparing a full second meal as with my freezer kit recipes, is an essential way to achieve a week of meals. But proper reheating can make or break your dinner. While a microwave can be quick and convenient, the food doesn't retain the texture and flavor you began with.

To reheat the recipes in this book, use the following methods.

CASSEROLES

In the oven: Preheat the oven to the original baking temperature and place the casserole, covered with a lid, on the center rack. Reheat until hot all the way through, 15 to 20 minutes.

PASTA OR POTATO DISHES

On the stovetop: Reheat pasta and potato dishes in a saucepan over medium heat, adding a little water or broth to maintain moisture and prevent sticking. If you plan to make a pasta dish in advance and refrigerate or freeze it, undercook the noodles slightly so they do not become mushy when reheated.

PIZZA

In the oven or toaster oven: Reheat slices or whole pizzas directly on the oven rack at 400°F, with a baking sheet placed on the rack below to catch drips. This method helps the pizza retain the crispness of its crust while reheating the toppings.

PROTEINS

In the oven: Preheat to 350°F and place your protein (meatballs, chicken thighs, and so on) on a baking sheet. Heat until warmed through. For proteins like meatloaf or steak, which are prone to drying out, fill a baking dish with ½ cup broth, water, or sauce and place the protein in the dish. Cover tightly and heat in a 300°F oven until warmed through.

On the stovetop: Reheat in a skillet over low heat. Add a splash of broth, water, or sauce to prevent sticking and maintain moisture.

SANDWICHES AND QUESADILLAS

On the stovetop: Reheat in a skillet over medium-low heat until the fillings are warm or melted and the tortilla or bread is crispy.

SKILLET OR SHEET-PAN MEALS

In the oven: Preheat to 350°F and place the contents on a baking sheet. Cover to preserve moisture and heat until warmed through.

On the stovetop: Place the contents in a dry skillet and reheat over low heat. Add a splash of broth, water, or sauce if it begins to stick.

SOUPS AND STEWS

On the stovetop: Reheat soups and stews in a saucepan over low to medium heat. Stir frequently to ensure even heating and to prevent sticking on the bottom of the pan. Soups and stews can become thick once they've been frozen or refrigerated, so add a splash of broth or water to thin it to your desired consistency. Taste and season the soup again, if necessary, after adding any liquid.

GENERAL REHEATING TIPS

Store leftovers properly in airtight containers in the refrigerator or freezer to maintain quality. Allowing foods to come to room temperature before storing prevents condensation from forming on the container, which can make leftovers soggy or too watery.

Defrost frozen meals in the refrigerator before reheating, unless you are using an Instant Pot, as this ensures even heating throughout.

Stir or flip the food occasionally during reheating to promote even distribution of heat.

A spritz of vinegar or lemon juice can help liven up flavors that seem to have dissipated with storage.

If your reheated dish lacks the desired texture, try briefly crisping it up in a hot, dry skillet or under the broiler in the oven.

When reheating a large batch of food, divide it into smaller portions for more efficient and even heating.

Experiment with adding herbs and spices to reheated meals for vibrancy and fresh flavor.

How a Well-Stocked Pantry Leads to Easy, Back-Pocket Dinners

A well-stocked pantry and freezer are essential cornerstones for efficient menu and budget planning, impromptu meals, and creative cooking. The nonperishable items in your pantry and the frozen goods in your freezer are the building blocks of what I call back-pocket dinners. These are recipes that rely on ingredients you probably already have in your pantry and frozen items you can stock up on easily.

Incorporating one or two of these quick recipes (see page 231) into your weekly meal plan will save you time, effort, and the stress of making last-minute grocery runs. They come in handy for those nights you had planned to go to the store but ran out of time, got back from work or a kid's sporting event late, or spent the day prepping sauces and individual ingredients but didn't plan for a full meal. With a few staple ingredients, such as jarred beans, grain-free pasta, jarred and frozen vegetables, and spices, you can create a variety of satisfying and nutritious dishes, eliminating the need to rely on takeout or prepackaged meals and giving you control over your ingredients and flavors. Note: There are two back-pocket dinners, my Sausage Skillets, Four Ways (page 240) and Four Quick-Grilled Chicken Marinades (page 247), that may require adding a few things to your shopping list for the week or foraging in your fridge and freezer for substitutes.

Back-pocket dinners also tend to be cost-effective. By using ingredients you already have in your pantry and freezer, you reduce your new-grocery expenses. This approach is particularly helpful when fresh ingredients are not readily available or affordable or when you're trying to stick to a budget.

I suggest that you integrate a back-pocket dinner into your menu plan toward the end of the week so you can also forage through your fridge for any leftover ingredients. A few fresh herbs or a squeeze of fresh lemon juice can do wonders! You will see that I've chosen one back-pocket dinner per week in the fifteen weekly meal plans. However, as mentioned, I did not include the ingredients for these in the grocery lists because you will probably already have everything you need on hand (that's especially true if you follow my advice below). So, feel free to swap these recipes around, modify them, or eliminate them altogether and opt for a freezer kit or even takeout when you need a break from the kitchen.

With that, let's talk about what you should regularly have in your freezer, fridge, and pantry. If you're new to eating paleo or gluten-free, some of these items may be unfamiliar, but fear not, since I have designed these recipes to use each ingredient to its fullest potential. And if you're a seasoned cook in this lifestyle, you likely have most (or all) of these items already.

Also see shop.daniellewalker.com for an updated list of my favorite and trusted brands.

FRIDGE AND PANTRY

Baking Ingredients

- Almond flour (blanched)
- Arrowroot powder (also called arrowroot flour)
- Baking mix (grain-free; vanilla cake or cupcake and pancake)
- Baking powder (grain-free)
- Baking soda
- Cacao powder (raw)
- Chocolate (dark; 85% cacao)
- Coconut flour
- Cream of tartar
- Honey (creamy, light-colored, raw)
- Maple sugar
- Maple syrup (pure)
- Palm sugar
- Vanilla extract (pure)

Canned, Jarred, and Boxed Ingredients

- Applesauce (unsweetened)
- BBQ sauce (unsweetened)
- Bone broth (chicken and beef, unsalted or low-sodium)
- Capers
- Cassava pasta
- Chickpea pasta
- Coconut aminos
- Coconut cream
- Coconut milk (full-fat; canned)
- Curry paste
- Enchilada sauce
- Fish (tuna, salmon, and sardines; tinned)
- Fish sauce
- Fruit preserves (unsweetened or sweetened with fruit juices)
- Ketchup (unsweetened)
- Lemon juice
- Liquid smoke (all-natural)
- Marinara sauce (free of soy, sugar, and preservatives)
- Mayonnaise (made with avocado oil)
- Olives
- Pickles
- Pineapple chunks
- Pumpkin puree
- Shirataki noodles
- Tomato products (no citric acid or sugars added, preferably in a jar or BPA-free box)

Oils and Vinegars

- Avocado oil
- Coconut oil (virgin or expeller-pressed for mild flavor)
- Ghee
- Olive oil (extra-virgin)
- Palm shortening (sustainable)
- Sesame oil (toasted)
- Apple cider vinegar
- Balsamic vinegar
- Red wine vinegar
- Rice vinegar (unseasoned, organic)
- White wine vinegar

Snacks and Spreads

- Almond butter (creamy, unsweetened)
- Almonds
- Cashew butter (raw)
- Cashews (raw)
- Coconut flakes (toasted, unsweetened)
- Crackers (grain-free)
- Flaxseeds
- Hazelnuts
- Macadamia nuts
- Pecans
- Pepitas (pumpkin seeds)
- Pine nuts
- Pistachios
- Plantain chips
- Potato chips (fried with avocado oil)
- Sesame seeds
- Sunflower seed butter
- Sunflower seeds (sprouted)
- Tahini
- Taro vegetable chips
- Tortilla chips (grain-free)
- Walnuts

Seasonings and Salt

- Nutritional yeast
- Organic seasonings and spices (your favorite types)
- Sea salt (coarse, typically Maldon or Fleur de Sel)
- Salt (fine; Celtic sea salt or pink Himalayan)

FREEZER

- Beef (grass-fed ground beef, steaks, or roasts)
- Bone broth (see also Canned, Jarred, and Boxed Ingredients)
- Cauliflower rice
- Chicken (organic; ground and boneless, skinless breasts and thighs)
- Flours (grain-free; see also Baking Ingredients)
- Freezer kits, such as Sheet-Pan Chicken Fajitas (page 177) and Italian Cottage Pie (page 149), gnocchi, or fresh pasta (grain-free)
- Herbs (freeze fresh herbs like basil, rosemary, or cilantro in ice cube trays with olive oil)
- Pizza crust (look for paleo-friendly, grain-free crusts made with almond, chickpea, or cassava flour)
- Sauces, such as Dairy-Free Pesto (page 32), Granny's Meat Sauce (see page 144), and Green Goddess Dressing (page 33)
- Sausages and hot dogs
- Seafood (wild-caught salmon, cod, shrimp, or other fish fillets)
- Soup (individual portions)
- Vegetables (broccoli, cauliflower, mirepoix mix, peas, potato or root vegetable hash browns, stir-fry vegetables, and spinach)

HEALTHY IN A HURRY SEASONINGS

While not essential to make any of the recipes in this book, I call for my gluten-free and organic-certified seasoning blends in some recipes to cut down on the number of ingredients (and measuring spoons!). Every jar is specially formulated and tested in my own kitchen, so you can create dishes that are as close to mine as possible.

You may not know this, because I didn't until I created these blends, but every bottle of chile powder on the market has a variation of smokiness; cayenne can be mild or red-hot; and the grind of onion powder can be coarse or fine. While store-bought spices and seasonings absolutely work and will not make a recipe fail, these variances can cause your homemade blends to greatly differ in taste and texture from my own. Plus, a lot of blends and seasonings include hidden sugars and anti-caking agents like rice starch, are processed on equipment where wheat is present, and often are not tested for pesticides and heavy metals.

My blends are Whole30 approved, gluten-free certified, and celiac safe, processed on equipment that is free of the top allergens, and tested for heavy metals. While these provide the most convenient and accurate way to mimic the flavors I create in my own kitchen, the recipes to mix up your own bottles of these blends are on pages 36–37.

Cooking Tools and Small Appliances That Make Meal Prep Simple

When it comes to stocking your kitchen for menu planning and meal prepping, there are several tools that will greatly enhance your efficiency and versatility. You may already have many of these in your kitchen, but if not, they would be good investments toward your meal-prepping success.

Chef's knife: A high-quality, sharp chef's knife is a must-have for chopping, slicing, and dicing ingredients with ease. Dull knives can slow you down, so whether you have a quality Japanese knife or a cost-effective one from Target, the key is to keep it sharp. Your local farmers' market or kitchen store will likely sharpen them for a small fee. I sharpen mine every 3 to 4 months, but 6 months is average.

Cutting board: Invest in a durable cutting board to protect your countertops and provide a stable surface for food preparation. A wood block such as Boos lasts a long time and is nontoxic. Be sure to keep it well oiled. If you cut raw meat on it frequently, let it sit in the sun for a day after cleaning it well with soap and water to kill any remaining bacteria.

Food processor: While not necessary, this versatile appliance can quickly chop, shred, and puree ingredients, making meal prep more efficient. If your space and budget are limited, try a 4-cup mini prep machine for chopping vegetables and whipping up sauces.

High-speed blender: Grain-free and dairy-free cooking requires extra preparation, and having a good blender can save you a lot of time. I use mine to create smooth doughs and batters, puree soups, and whip up smoothies. A regular blender works just fine in these recipes but may require you to blend for a longer duration and occasionally stop the machine to scrape down the sides.

Mason jars with spout lids: Do yourself a favor and purchase a pack of spout lids for your wide-mouth and standard-size mason jars. They turn a simple jar into the best vessel for pouring salad dressings, homemade coffee creamer, and nut milks without the drips. You can find them on shop.daniellewalker.com or Amazon.

Mixing bowls: When you're prepping components in advance, having a stack of assorted mixing bowls is essential for combining ingredients, marinating, and storing prepped items. Look for ones with lids, so you can easily stack them in the fridge.

Parchment paper or silicone mats: Lining a roasting pan or sheet pan with parchment paper before cooking makes for easy cleanup and keeps heavy metals such as aluminum from touching your food. Covering the bottom of cake and loaf pans with a piece of parchment helps your cakes and breads slip out easily after baking.

Pans: Saucepan (3 quarts); stockpot (8 quarts); Dutch oven (5 to 7 quarts); sauté pan or skillet (14 inches). I frequently use a 14-inch skillet in these recipes so the food browns evenly and doesn't overcrowd the pan. Smaller skillets will work but may also overflow the pan in recipes that serve more than six people. Switch to a Dutch oven if this is the case.

Recycled ghee jars: Yes, these get their very own category since I use them so often. I fill them with homemade nut milks, single-serving portions of soups to freeze and reheat quickly when one of us is under the weather, sauces, nuts and seeds, and even a small salad to take on the road.

Sheet pans and baking sheets: These versatile pans are ideal for roasting vegetables, baking cookies, and preparing sheet-pan meals. When I call for a full sheet pan in a recipe, I'm talking about a rimmed baking sheet that measures roughly 18 by 26 inches. This large size keeps food from steaming due to overcrowding and browns and cooks evenly. If you have a small oven, divide the ingredients between two half sheet pans (roughly 18 by 13 inches each) and rotate midway through cooking.

Silicone muffin molds: For freezing soups, broth, sauces, cake batter (yes, you can!; see page 20), and even for my dairy-free Cheesy Nacho Sauce (page 218), I use 6-cavity jumbo silicone muffin pans. The cavities are 3½ inches wide and hold roughly 1 cup of liquid each. Freezing in small quantities not only saves space in the freezer but also makes defrosting quick and reheating customizable to the number of people I'm serving or what I need the ingredient for.

Slow cooker and/or Instant Pot: These appliances are excellent for batch cooking because they allow you to prepare large quantities of food with minimal effort. My recipes that call for them typically have interchangeable instructions or stovetop instructions. I use a 6-quart Instant Pot and a 6.5-quart slow cooker.

Storage containers: Opt for airtight containers in different sizes to efficiently store prepped ingredients and leftovers. See page 18 for more information on the ones I use.

Basic Prep Recipes

Dairy-Free Ranch Dressing

MAKES 2 CUPS
ACTIVE TIME: 8 MINUTES

1 cup avocado oil mayonnaise

½ cup full-fat coconut milk

¼ cup chopped flat-leaf parsley

2 garlic cloves, minced

2 tablespoons chopped chives

2 tablespoons chopped dill

4 teaspoons fresh lemon juice

½ teaspoon onion powder

½ teaspoon fine sea salt

In a medium bowl, whisk together all the ingredients, mixing well. Store in an airtight container in the refrigerator up to 2 weeks.

MAKE AHEAD

Mix the coconut milk, parsley, garlic, chives, dill, lemon juice, onion powder, and salt in a medium bowl. Divide into three silicone muffin molds, cover, and freeze. For ½ cup dressing: Defrost one puck (see page 20) in a bowl at room temperature for 30 minutes, then whisk in ⅓ cup mayonnaise.

Dairy-Free Pesto

MAKES ⅓ CUP
ACTIVE TIME: 10 MINUTES

⅓ cup pine nuts, lightly toasted

3 cups tightly packed basil leaves

3 garlic cloves

1 teaspoon fresh lemon juice

½ teaspoon fine sea salt

⅓ cup extra-virgin olive oil, plus more for storing

In a food processor or blender, combine the pine nuts, basil, garlic, lemon juice, and salt and pulse until finely chopped. With the machine running, slowly drizzle in the oil and process until a pourable paste forms. Continue to process for about 15 seconds more, until smooth. Use immediately or store in an airtight container in the refrigerator.

MAKE AHEAD

Transfer the pesto to a storage container and gently drizzle a thin layer of oil evenly over the top. The oil prevents air from reaching the pesto, keeping it green. Cover tightly and store in the refrigerator up to 3 weeks or freeze up to 6 months. Replace the thin layer of oil every time you use it and return the container to the refrigerator to keep it fresh.

Green Goddess Dressing

MAKES 2 CUPS
ACTIVE TIME: 10 MINUTES

4-ounces soft dairy-free goat cheese

¾ cup unsweetened cashew milk

¼ cup extra-virgin olive oil

Zest and juice of 1 lemon

2 garlic cloves

1½ cups packed mixed fresh herbs, such as dill, tarragon, parsley, basil, or mint

1 small bunch chives

1½ teaspoons sea salt

¼ teaspoon cracked black pepper

In a blender or using a jar and immersion blender, blend goat cheese, cashew milk, olive oil, lemon zest and juice, garlic, herbs, chives, salt, and black pepper until smooth and creamy. Store in refrigerator up to 2 weeks.

Stir-Fry Sauce

MAKES 2½ CUPS
ACTIVE TIME: 5 MINUTES

2 cups coconut aminos

2 tablespoons plus 2 teaspoons fish sauce

2 tablespoons plus 2 teaspoons toasted sesame oil

1 tablespoon unseasoned rice vinegar, or 1½ teaspoons apple cider vinegar

1½ teaspoons fine sea salt

1 teaspoon white pepper

In a large jar, combine all the ingredients. Cap tightly and shake vigorously to mix well. Store in the refrigerator up to 3 months.

Dairy-Free Parmesan Cheese

MAKES 1 CUP
ACTIVE TIME: 8 MINUTES

¾ cup whole raw cashews

2½ tablespoons nutritional yeast

¾ teaspoon fine sea salt

½ teaspoon garlic powder

Place all the ingredients in a food processor and process until it has the texture of fine sand. Store in an airtight jar in the refrigerator up to 3 months.

Ginger-Sesame Dressing

MAKES 3 CUPS
ACTIVE TIME: 12 MINUTES

⅓ cup toasted sesame oil

½ cup coconut aminos

½ cup unseasoned rice vinegar

¼ cup honey

8 garlic cloves

2-inch piece ginger

2 tablespoons tahini

¼ teaspoon cayenne pepper

¾ cup avocado oil

In the jar of a blender, combine the sesame oil, coconut aminos, vinegar, honey, garlic, ginger, tahini, and cayenne. Secure the lid and blend on high until smooth. Add the avocado oil and blend again for 30 seconds. Refrigerate up to 2 weeks.

Make-Ahead Meatballs

MAKES 50 MEATBALLS
ACTIVE TIME: 50 MINUTES

LAMB

3 pounds lean ground lamb

½ cup dairy-free unsweetened yogurt

1 head garlic, cloves peeled and minced (about ¼ cup)

2 teaspoons sea salt

2 teaspoons cracked black pepper

1 tablespoon onion powder

1 tablespoon ground cumin

2 cups chopped fresh herbs (such as cilantro, mint, dill, basil, or parsley)

CHICKEN

2 tablespoons extra-virgin olive oil

3 pounds ground chicken

2 eggs

3 tablespoons mayonnaise

½ cup almond flour, or 2 tablespoons coconut flour

2 teaspoons sea salt

1 teaspoon garlic powder

1 teaspoon onion powder

¼ teaspoon cracked black pepper

BEEF

3 eggs

3 pounds ground beef

¾ cup almond flour, or 3 tablespoons coconut flour

3 tablespoons nutritional yeast, or ⅓ cup sheep's milk Pecorino Romano

3 garlic cloves, minced

1 tablespoon coconut aminos

1½ teaspoons sea salt

1½ teaspoons fish sauce

¼ teaspoon red pepper flakes

TURKEY

3 pounds ground turkey

2 eggs

½ cup chopped baby spinach

¼ cup grated yellow onion

¼ cup chopped parsley

1½ teaspoons garlic powder

1 teaspoon onion powder

1 teaspoon sea salt

½ teaspoon cracked black pepper

2 tablespoons extra-virgin olive oil, ghee, or coconut oil

In a large bowl, mix together all ingredients. Using a 1½-tablespoon cookie scoop, scoop out even portions of mixture onto a large plate, making about fifty meatballs. With wet hands for easier handling, shape each portion into a round meatball.

Oven: Set an oven rack on second-to-top position and preheat oven to 400°F. Line a half sheet pan with parchment paper. Place a cooling rack on top of parchment and lightly rub the rack with a bit of olive oil.

Working in two batches, arrange meatballs on cooling rack in a single layer; if meatballs gently touch, that's okay. Bake for 15 minutes, then increase oven temperature to broil. Broil for 3 to 5 minutes to brown, then flip and broil for 1 to 2 minutes longer. Remove meatballs and repeat with remaining mixture.

Pan-fry: In a large, lidded skillet over medium-high heat, warm oil until it shimmers and becomes fragrant, about 2 minutes. Working in batches, add meatballs in a single layer and cook, turning frequently, until golden brown, about 5 minutes. If oil becomes too hot, turn heat to medium. Add ¼ cup water to bottom of skillet, cover with lid, and cook meatballs until cooked through, 2 to 3 minutes longer. Using a slotted spoon, transfer meatballs to a serving plate. Repeat with remaining meatballs.

MAKE AHEAD

Refrigerate, uncooked, up to 3 days; cooked, up to 1 week

Freeze, cooked, up to 4 months; uncooked, up to 6 months

NOTES AND SHORTCUTS

Speed up the process by mincing or grating ingredients like garlic and onions in a food processor or mini prep processor.

HEALTHY IN A HURRY SEASONING BLENDS

Find my entire line to purchase at healthyinahurry.com.

Adobo Seasoning

MAKES 1 CUP

¼ cup fine sea salt

¼ cup garlic powder

2 tablespoons dried oregano

2 tablespoons onion powder

1½ tablespoons ground cumin

1 tablespoon cracked black pepper

2 teaspoons annatto powder or ground turmeric

In a bowl, stir together all the ingredients, mixing well. Store in an airtight container in the pantry up to 6 months.

BBQ Rub

MAKES 1 CUP

¼ cup sweet paprika

¼ cup chili powder

2 tablespoons fine sea salt

1 tablespoon garlic powder

1 tablespoon dry mustard

2 teaspoons dried oregano

2 teaspoons ground cumin

¾ teaspoon cracked black pepper

½ teaspoon cayenne pepper

In a bowl, stir together all the ingredients, mixing well. Store in an airtight container in the pantry up to 6 months.

Burnt Broccoli Seasoning

MAKES ½ CUP

3 tablespoons fine sea salt

2 tablespoons garlic powder

1 tablespoon chili powder

1 tablespoon ground cumin

1 tablespoon onion powder

1½ teaspoons ground cinnamon

1½ teaspoons ground coriander

1½ teaspoons cracked black pepper

In a bowl, stir together all the ingredients, mixing well. Store in an airtight container in the pantry up to 6 months.

Fries Seasoning Salt

MAKES ⅓ CUP

2 tablespoons fine sea salt

1 tablespoon smoked paprika

1 tablespoon garlic powder

1½ teaspoons onion powder

1½ teaspoons chili powder

1½ teaspoons dried basil

¾ teaspoon ground cumin

¾ teaspoon ground sage

¾ teaspoon cracked black pepper

¼ teaspoon dried oregano

In a bowl, stir together all the ingredients, mixing well. Store in an airtight container in the pantry up to 6 months.

Taco Seasoning

MAKES 2 CUPS

½ cup plus
2 tablespoons chili
powder

⅓ cup fine sea salt

⅓ cup ground cumin

¼ cup dried oregano

2½ tablespoons
onion powder

2½ tablespoons
ground coriander

2½ tablespoons
sweet paprika

1 teaspoon cayenne
pepper (see Note)

1 teaspoon cracked
black pepper

In a bowl, stir together all the ingredients, mixing well. Store in an airtight container in the pantry up to 6 months.

Note: Use up to 3 teaspoons cayenne if you want this to be spicy.

Cajun Seasoning

MAKES 1 CUP

¼ cup smoked paprika

2 tablespoons onion
powder

2 tablespoons garlic
powder

4 teaspoons dried
oregano

4 teaspoons dried
thyme

4 teaspoons fine
sea salt

2 teaspoons cracked
black pepper

1 teaspoon cayenne
pepper (see Note)

1 teaspoon dry
mustard

1 teaspoon red
pepper flakes

In a bowl, stir together all the ingredients, mixing well. Store in an airtight container in the pantry up to 6 months.

Note: Use up to 2 teaspoons cayenne if you want this to be spicy.

Mediterranean Seasoning

MAKES 1¾ CUPS

¼ cup garlic powder

¼ cup dried oregano

¼ cup dried marjoram

¼ cup dried rosemary

¼ cup dried thyme

¼ cup cracked
black pepper

4 teaspoons dried dill

4 teaspoons fine
sea salt

1 teaspoon ground
nutmeg

1 teaspoon ground
cinnamon

In a spice grinder or a clean coffee grinder, combine all the ingredients and grind to a fine powder. Store in an airtight container in the pantry up to 6 months.

Tagine Seasoning

MAKES 1¾ CUPS

¼ cup ground cumin

¼ cup ground coriander

2½ tablespoons fine
sea salt

2 tablespoons ground
cinnamon

1 tablespoon plus
1 teaspoon ground
ginger

1 tablespoon plus
1 teaspoon ground
turmeric

1 tablespoon ground
nutmeg

1 tablespoon cracked
black pepper

2 teaspoons ground
allspice

2 teaspoons cayenne
pepper

In a bowl, stir together all the ingredients, mixing well. Store in an airtight container in the pantry up to 6 months.

Part 2

15 Weeks of Meal Plans

Week 1

1

This week's meal plan is a perfect blend of convenience and versatility. If you're having a busy week, my shortcuts will help. And if you're a Freezer Prepper, you'll like the option to double up on both the meatballs and the soup and stash them for future meals.

I call for a store-bought rotisserie chicken for the soup and the brussels salad, which is a quick-and-easy base. And while I try to keep homemade meatballs in my freezer at all times, go ahead and take a shortcut this week by purchasing your favorite store-bought brand.

I recommend the tuna casserole as your back-pocket dinner this week to use up the celery you bought for the salad. And you can sprinkle any leftover green onions over the top.

MAKE AHEAD

UP TO 1 WEEK

- Make meatballs (if using homemade)
- Make grits for Cajun steak
- Make teriyaki sauce for meatballs
- Make cauliflower rice for meatballs

UP TO 3 DAYS

- Rub London broil with Cajun seasoning
- Pan-fry bacon and make bacon vinaigrette

UP TO 1 DAY

- Thaw meatballs in refrigerator

PREP AHEAD

- Shred brussels sprouts
- Wash and tear frisée lettuce
- Shred rotisserie chicken
- Chop 5 celery stalks
- Dice 2 yellow onions
- Shred carrots
- Chop bell peppers
- Mince 6 garlic cloves
- Slice green onion (white and green parts separated)

GROCERY LIST

PROTEIN

- London broil **2 pounds**
- Shredded rotisserie chicken **4½ cups**
- Thick-cut sugar- and nitrate-free bacon **4 slices**

PRODUCE

- Brussels sprouts **12 ounces**
- Carrots **9**
- Cauliflower rice **for serving**
- Celery stalks **5**
- Curly kale **4 cups**
- Frisée lettuce **3 cups**
- Garlic cloves **6**
- Green onion **1**
- Multicolored bell peppers **6**
- Tart apple **1**
- Yellow onions **2**

REFRIGERATOR

- Cashew milk **4 cups**

FREEZER

- Frozen cooked chicken or beef meatballs (see page 34) **3 pounds**
- Grain-free gnocchi **2 (10- to 12-ounce) packages**

CUPBOARD & COUNTER

- Almond flour **2½ cups**
- Apple cider vinegar **4½ tablespoons**
- Arrowroot powder **2 tablespoons**
- Coconut aminos **¼ cup**
- Dijon mustard **1 tablespoon**
- Dried thyme **2 teaspoons**
- Ground ginger **1 teaspoon**
- Healthy in a Hurry Cajun Seasoning (page 37) **2½ tablespoons**
- Hot sauce **(optional)**
- Nutritional yeast **1½ tablespoons**
- Pineapple chunks **2 (14-ounce) cans**
- Pure maple syrup **2 teaspoons**
- Red wine vinegar **2½ tablespoons**
- Tomato paste **2 tablespoons**
- Unsalted chicken bone broth **6 (16-ounce) containers**
- Unsweetened apricot jam **1 (10-ounce) jar**
- Unsweetened cashew butter **¼ cup**
- Unsweetened paleo-friendly ketchup **1 cup**

Brussels and Apple Salad
with Bacon Vinaigrette

¼ cup, plus 1 tablespoon
extra-virgin olive oil

12 ounces brussels sprouts,
thinly shredded

4 slices thick-cut sugar-
and nitrate-free bacon

2 tablespoons red wine vinegar

1 tablespoon Dijon mustard

2 teaspoons pure maple syrup

Sea salt and cracked
black pepper

3 cups coarsely torn
frisée lettuce

1½ cups shredded
rotisserie chicken

1 tart apple, thinly sliced

In a large skillet over medium heat, warm 1 tablespoon oil until it shimmers. Add brussels sprouts and sauté for 5 to 7 minutes, until tender but still crisp. Remove to a plate and wipe pan clean.

Line a plate with paper towels.

Add bacon to clean pan, turn heat to medium-high, and pan-fry until crisp. Using tongs, transfer bacon to prepared plate to drain, leaving grease in pan.

Add vinegar, mustard, and maple syrup to pan and whisk until smooth and combined. Gradually pour in remaining ¼ cup oil, whisking constantly until smooth. Season with salt and pepper.

Chop bacon.

In a large bowl, toss together frisée, brussels sprouts, chicken, bacon, and apples. Drizzle with half of warm dressing and toss again to coat.

Serve salad immediately, with remaining dressing alongside.

1

SERVES 4 TO 6
ACTIVE TIME: 18 MINUTES

PREP AHEAD

Shred brussels sprouts

Shred chicken

Slice apple

MAKE AHEAD

Refrigerate salad dressing
separately, up to 1 week

NOTES AND SHORTCUTS

Purchase pre-shredded
brussels sprouts or shred
using food processor fitted
with grater attachment

Sub sautéed shrimp for
chicken

1

PREP AHEAD

Chop celery

Mince garlic

Dice onion

Shred carrots

Shred rotisserie chicken

MAKE AHEAD

Refrigerate up to 1 week

Freeze up to 4 months

NOTES AND SHORTCUTS

Capello's and Trader Joe's offer grain-free and gluten-free gnocchi

Sub diced potatoes for gnocchi

Sub 4 cups coconut milk, whisked with ⅓ cup garbanzo bean flour for cashew milk

Sub any cooked chicken for rotisserie

Omit chicken for vegetarian

Creamy Gnocchi Soup

4 cups cashew milk

2 tablespoons arrowroot powder

¼ cup extra-virgin olive oil

3 celery stalks, chopped

1 yellow onion, diced

4 garlic cloves, minced

2 (10- to 12-ounce) packages grain-free gnocchi

4 (16-ounce) containers unsalted chicken bone broth

3 cups shredded carrots

1 teaspoon apple cider vinegar

2 teaspoons dried thyme

1½ teaspoons sea salt

½ teaspoon cracked black pepper

3 cups shredded rotisserie chicken

4 cups curly kale, coarsely chopped

Make one batch to cook now and a second batch to freeze for later.

In a bowl, whisk together cashew milk and arrowroot until smooth.

In a Dutch oven over medium heat or in an Instant Pot set to sauté mode high, warm the oil until it shimmers. Add celery, onion, and garlic and sauté for 3 to 5 minutes, until onion is translucent. Move vegetables to side and add gnocchi. Brown well, about 5 minutes. Transfer half this mixture and half the cashew milk mixture to a 9-inch glass container or freezer bag; leave remaining mixture in pot.

TO COOK NOW

Stovetop: Add 2 containers broth and remaining cashew milk mixture to Dutch oven. Equally divide carrots, vinegar, thyme, salt, and black pepper between Dutch oven and freezer container. Bring Dutch oven mixture to a boil over medium-high heat, then turn heat to low and let simmer for 10 minutes, until carrots are tender.

Equally divide chicken and kale between Dutch oven and freezer container. Remove Dutch oven from heat. Seal freezer container and store in freezer for later.

Instant Pot: Add 2 containers broth and remaining cashew milk mixture to Instant Pot. Equally divide carrots, vinegar, thyme, salt, and black pepper between Instant Pot and freezer container. Secure lid and set valve to seal. Cook on high pressure with a 5-minute timer. Quick-release pressure.

Equally divide chicken and kale between Instant Pot and freezer container. Seal freezer container and store in freezer for later.

Season soup with salt and black pepper and serve hot.

TO COOK LATER

Remove container from freezer.

Stovetop: Once thawed completely, combine gnocchi mixture and 2 containers broth in Dutch oven and bring to a boil over medium-high heat, then turn heat to low and let simmer for 10 minutes, until carrots are tender and broth has thickened. Serve as directed above.

Instant Pot: Once thawed just enough to remove contents, add gnocchi mixture to Instant Pot, secure lid, and set valve to seal. Cook on high pressure with a 20-minute timer. Quick-release pressure. Serve as directed above.

1

PREP AHEAD

Whisk sauce

Tear bell peppers

MAKE AHEAD

Refrigerate, cooked, up to
1 week; uncooked, up to
3 days

Freeze up to 4 months

Make meatballs up to
4 months

NOTES AND SHORTCUTS

Meatball brands: Amylu
Foods, Aidells, Cooked
Perfect, Sprouts, Trader
Joe's

It's important to use canned
pineapple instead of fresh
here. The enzymes in
fresh pineapple are much
stronger and can cause
the proteins in the meat
to break down too much,
causing mushy meatballs.

Sub 3 cups BBQ sauce for
teriyaki sauce

St. Dalfour makes a fruit-
sweetened apricot jam

If cooking for a smaller
crowd, divide freezer kits
into three or four containers

Teriyaki Meatballs

1 cup unsweetened
paleo-friendly ketchup

2 (14-ounce) cans pineapple
chunks, drained and juice
reserved

1 (10-ounce) jar unsweetened
apricot jam

¼ cup apple cider vinegar

¼ cup coconut aminos

1 teaspoon ground ginger

3 pounds frozen cooked chicken
or beef meatballs (see page 34)

4 multicolored bell peppers,
seeded and coarsely cut into
2-inch chunks

Cauliflower rice for serving

Make one batch to cook now and a second batch to freeze for later.

In a large bowl, whisk together ketchup, ½ cup reserved pineapple
juice, jam, vinegar, coconut aminos, and ginger. Stir in meatballs,
pineapple chunks, and bell peppers.

Place half this mixture in a 9-inch glass container or freezer bag and
seal. Store in freezer for later.

TO COOK NOW

Instant Pot: Place remaining mixture in an Instant Pot. Secure lid
and set valve to seal. Cook on high pressure with a 3-minute timer.
Let pressure release naturally for 10 minutes. Quick-release any
remaining pressure. If desired, transfer machine to sauté mode high
to thicken sauce.

Slow Cooker: Place remaining mixture in a slow cooker and cook
on low for 4 hours or high for 2 hours.

Serve hot over cauliflower rice.

TO COOK LATER

Instant Pot: Remove container from freezer and allow to thaw just
enough to remove contents. Add ¼ cup water and cook as directed
above but use a 5-minute timer.

Slow Cooker: Remove container from freezer and allow to thaw
completely. Cook as directed above.

Cajun Steak and Cheesy Almond Grits

2 pounds London broil, cut into thirds

2½ tablespoons Healthy in a Hurry Cajun Seasoning (page 37)

2 tablespoons avocado oil

2 red or orange bell peppers, seeded and diced

2 celery stalks, diced

1 yellow onion, minced

1 green onion, white and green parts, trimmed and thinly sliced

2 garlic cloves, minced

2 tablespoons tomato paste

1 teaspoon red wine vinegar

½ teaspoon sea salt

¼ teaspoon cracked black pepper

CHEESY ALMOND GRITS

2¾ cups unsalted chicken bone broth

¼ cup unsweetened cashew butter

2½ cups almond flour

1½ tablespoons nutritional yeast

1 teaspoon sea salt

¼ teaspoon cracked black pepper

Hot sauce (optional)

SERVES 6
ACTIVE TIME: 25 MINUTES

PREP AHEAD

Dice bell peppers and celery

Mince yellow onion

Slice green onion

Mince garlic

MAKE AHEAD

Refrigerate up to 1 week

Freeze up to 4 months

NOTES AND SHORTCUTS

Sub flank steak or top round steak for London broil

Sub whitefish or salmon for steak

Sub ½ cup Kite Hill ricotta, shredded sheep's milk Pecorino

Sub Romano or sharp grass-fed Cheddar cheese for nutritional yeast

Sub ½ cup cashews blended into bone broth for cashew butter

Season both sides of London broil with Cajun seasoning.

In a large cast-iron skillet over medium-high heat, pan-fry steaks for 4 to 6 minutes per side, until an instant-read thermometer inserted into middle registers 135°F for medium-rare. Transfer steaks to a cutting board and lightly tent with parchment paper.

In same skillet over medium heat, warm oil until it shimmers. Add bell peppers, celery, yellow onion, white parts of green onion, and garlic and sauté for 8 to 10 minutes, until yellow onion is translucent. Stir in tomato paste, vinegar, salt, and pepper. Turn heat to low to keep warm.

Make grits: Meanwhile, In a medium saucepan over high heat, whisk together broth and cashew butter and bring to a boil. Turn heat to medium and whisk in almond flour and nutritional yeast. Bring mixture to a simmer and cook for 10 to 12 minutes, whisking constantly to prevent clumping, until thickened. Season with salt and pepper. Turn heat to low and keep warm.

Slice steaks against grain on a diagonal. Spoon grits into bowls and top with steak and a spoonful of vegetables. Sprinkle with green parts of green onion and drizzle with hot sauce, if desired, before serving.

Week 2

2

This week's meal plan calls for shortcut items like frozen meatballs, a delicious ginger dressing that can be made ahead and stored for weeks, and frozen cauliflower rice.

Put your food processor to work to chop herbs and vegetables, shred carrots, and even shred kale for the salad once you've removed the center ribs. You'll have to chop a daunting sixteen cloves of garlic to use throughout the week, so either quickly smash them with the butt of your knife to remove the peels and then use a food processor to chop them or purchase a bag of peeled cloves.

You'll use every last sprig of herbs in the kale salad, but if you happen to get extra-large bunches or have some left over from a previous grocery run, sprinkle them on top of the soup for added nutrients and a boost of fresh flavor for the gnocchi and sausage, if you choose to make it.

All these meals can be fully made in advance and stored as components for quick lunches or full meals if you're a Batch Cooker who wants to bang everything out over the weekend. To maximize your time, make a double batch of the soup, as it freezes brilliantly.

MAKE AHEAD

UP TO 1 WEEK
- Make meatballs (if using homemade)
- Make ginger-sesame dressing for meatballs
- Make lemon-garlic aioli for Spanish rice
- Build salads, with crunchy topping stored separately

UP TO 3 DAYS
- Brown bacon and sausage

UP TO 1 DAY
- Thaw meatballs in refrigerator

PREP AHEAD
- Peel and devein shrimp
- Cut broccoli into florets and peel and slice stems
- Slice green onions, white and green parts separated
- Trim and slice snap peas
- Dice 2 yellow onions
- Peel 16 garlic cloves
- Dice sweet potatoes
- Dice chorizo
- Shred kale
- Slice bell peppers
- Chop herbs

GROCERY LIST

PROTEIN

- Boneless skinless chicken breasts 3
- Jumbo shrimp ½ pound
- Bulk mild Italian sausage 1½ pounds
- Spanish chorizo 3 ounces
- Sugar- and nitrate-free bacon 1 (8-ounce) package

PRODUCE

- Baby spinach 5 ounces
- Broccoli 1 large head
- Carrots 3
- Fresh basil 1 bunch
- Fresh cilantro 1 bunch
- Fresh mint 1 bunch
- Fresh flat-leaf parsley 1 bunch (optional)
- Lemon 1
- Garlic cloves 16 (about 2 heads)
- Ginger 2-inch piece
- Green onions 4
- Kale 2 large bunches
- Large white-fleshed sweet potatoes 2
- Mung bean sprouts 1 (9-ounce) package
- Red bell peppers 2
- Sugar snap peas 8 ounces
- Yellow onions 2

REFRIGERATOR

- Cashew milk (or coconut cream) 1 cup

FREEZER

- Cooked frozen chicken or beef meatballs (see page 34) 1½ pounds
- Frozen cauliflower rice 2 (12-ounce) packages
- Frozen peas ¼ cup

CUPBOARD & COUNTER

- Arrowroot powder 1 teaspoon
- Avocado oil mayonnaise ¼ cup
- Cayenne pepper ¼ teaspoon
- Coconut aminos ½ cup
- Crushed red pepper flakes ½ teaspoon
- Diced tomatoes 1 (26-ounce) box
- Garlic powder ¼ teaspoon
- Ghee 3 tablespoons
- Ground turmeric ¾ teaspoon
- Honey ¼ cup
- Sesame seeds ½ teaspoon
- Smoked paprika ½ teaspoon
- Something crunchy and salty, such as grain-free french-fried onions 1 cup
- Tahini 2 tablespoons
- Toasted sesame oil ⅓ cup plus ½ teaspoon
- Unsalted chicken bone broth 6 cups
- Unseasoned rice vinegar ½ cup

2

PREP AHEAD

Dice onion and mince garlic

Peel and devein shrimp

Dice chorizo

MAKE AHEAD

Refrigerate aioli up to
1 week

Refrigerate rice up to 3 days

Freeze rice up to 3 months

NOTES AND SHORTCUTS

Sub avocado oil for ghee

Sub cooked short-grain
white rice for cauliflower
rice

Try Whole Foods Pilaf-
Style Riced Cauliflower
for added flavor

Sub 3 ounces pancetta
plus 1 teaspoon Healthy
in a Hurry Cajun Seasoning
(page 37) for chorizo

Spanish Rice with Chorizo, Artichokes, and Lemon-Garlic Aioli

3 tablespoons ghee

1 yellow onion, diced

4 garlic cloves, minced

½ pound jumbo shrimp,
peeled and deveined

3 ounces Spanish chorizo, diced

2 (12-ounce) packages frozen
cauliflower rice

¾ teaspoon ground turmeric

½ teaspoon smoked paprika

¾ teaspoon sea salt

¼ teaspoon cracked black pepper

1 (26-ounce) box diced tomatoes,
drained

¼ cup frozen peas

LEMON-GARLIC AIOLI

¼ cup avocado-oil mayonnaise

2 teaspoons fresh lemon juice

¼ teaspoon garlic powder

⅛ teaspoon sea salt

2 tablespoons chopped flat-leaf
parsley (optional)

In a large cast-iron skillet over medium heat, melt ghee. Add onion
and garlic and sauté for 7 to 10 minutes, until onion is translucent and
garlic is golden brown. Stir in shrimp and chorizo and cook, stirring
frequently, for 3 to 5 minutes, until shrimp are pink throughout. Add
cauliflower rice, turmeric, paprika, salt, and pepper and sauté for 3 to
5 minutes, until crisp-tender. Stir in tomatoes and peas, cover, and
steam for 5 minutes, until cauliflower rice is tender.

To make aioli: While rice steams, in a small bowl, whisk together
mayonnaise, lemon juice, garlic powder, and salt.

Serve rice, hot, with dollops of aioli and garnished with parsley,
if desired.

Ginger Meatballs
with Sesame Broccoli

GINGER-SESAME DRESSING

⅓ cup toasted sesame oil

½ cup coconut aminos

½ cup unseasoned rice vinegar

¼ cup honey

8 garlic cloves

2-inch piece ginger

2 tablespoons tahini

¼ teaspoon cayenne pepper

¾ cup avocado oil

2 tablespoons avocado oil

4 green onions, trimmed and thinly sliced, white and green parts separated

1½ pounds cooked frozen chicken or beef meatballs (see page 34)

2 cups water

1 large head broccoli, cut into florets and stems peeled and thinly sliced

½ teaspoon toasted sesame oil

½ teaspoon sesame seeds

½ teaspoon sea salt

8 ounces sugar snap peas, trimmed and thinly sliced on a diagonal

PREP AHEAD

Slice green onions, white and green parts separated.

Cut broccoli into florets and peel and slice stems

Trim and slice snap peas

MAKE AHEAD

Refrigerate dressing up to 2 weeks

Refrigerate up to 1 week

Freeze up to 4 months

Make meatballs up to 4 months

NOTES AND SHORTCUTS

Meatball brands: Amylu Foods, Aidells, Cooked Perfect, Sprouts, Trader Joe's

Sub SideDish or Primal Kitchen sauce for homemade

To make dressing: In jar of a blender, combine sesame oil, coconut aminos, vinegar, honey, garlic, ginger, tahini, and cayenne. Secure lid and blend on high speed until smooth. Add avocado oil and blend again for 30 seconds. Set aside.

In a large skillet over medium-high heat, warm avocado oil until it shimmers. Add white parts of green onions and meatballs and brown well on all sides, 4 to 6 minutes. Pour ½ cup of water into pan, then cover and steam for 5 minutes, until meatballs are thawed and warmed through.

Fill a medium pot with remaining 1½ cups water and put a steamer basket over water. Add broccoli, set over high heat, and bring water to a boil. Turn heat to medium-low and steam, covered, for 5 minutes or until crisp-tender.

Uncover meatballs and stir in ½ cup dressing. Remove from heat.

Drain water, remove basket, and return broccoli to pot. Toss broccoli with sesame oil, sesame seeds, and salt.

Serve sauced meatballs with sesame broccoli, snap peas, and green parts of green onions.

2

PREP AHEAD

Dice onion

Mince garlic

Brown bacon and sausage

Dice sweet potatoes

MAKE AHEAD

Refrigerate up to 5 days

Freeze up to 6 months

NOTES AND SHORTCUTS

Sub russet potatoes or celeriac for sweet potatoes

Use spicy Italian sausage, if preferred

Eliminate red pepper flakes for a milder soup

Sub heavy cream for cashew milk

Creamy Sausage and Potato Soup

1½ pounds bulk mild Italian sausage

1 (8-ounce) package sugar- and nitrate-free bacon, chopped

½ teaspoon crushed red pepper flakes

1 medium yellow onion, diced

4 garlic cloves, minced

6 cups unsalted chicken bone broth

2 large white-fleshed sweet potatoes, peeled and diced

1 cup cashew milk or coconut cream

1 teaspoon arrowroot powder

5 ounces baby spinach, coarsely chopped

In a large Dutch oven over medium-high heat, cook sausage, bacon, and red pepper flakes for 5 to 7 minutes, until well browned. Using a slotted spoon, drain sausage and bacon on a paper towel–lined plate. Leave 2 tablespoons grease in pan and discard remaining.

Add onion and garlic to Dutch oven and sauté until softened and browned, about 5 minutes. Pour in broth and add sweet potatoes. Turn heat to low, cover, and let simmer for 10 to 12 minutes, until potatoes are fork-tender.

In a small bowl, whisk together cashew milk and arrowroot powder and add to pot. Turn heat to high and bring soup to boil and thicken for 5 minutes. Remove from heat and stir in sausage, bacon, and spinach.

Serve hot.

Herby Kale Salad with Ginger-Sesame Dressing

3 boneless, skinless chicken breasts

¾ cup Ginger-Sesame Dressing (page 33)

¼ cup avocado oil

8 cups shredded kale, ribs and stems removed

2 cups shredded carrots

2 red bell peppers, seeded and thinly sliced

1 (9-ounce) package mung bean sprouts

½ cup packed chopped cilantro leaves and tender stems

½ cup chopped mint

½ cup chopped basil

Sea salt and cracked black pepper

1 cup something crunchy and salty, such as grain-free french-fried onions, chopped dry-roasted cashews, or sprouted sunflower seeds

Place chicken in a resealable bag and add ¼ cup of dressing and avocado oil over top. Seal and refrigerate for at least 6 hours or—better yet—overnight.

In a large bowl, drizzle ½ cup of dressing over kale and toss with your hands to massage dressing into greens. If eating now, top kale with carrots, bell peppers, sprouts, cilantro, mint, and basil. If saving for later, divide the ingredients equally into six medium containers.

Prepare a grill for medium heat.

Remove chicken from marinade and scrape off any excess. Season with salt and pepper and grill for 5 to 6 minutes per side, until an instant-read thermometer inserted into center registers 165°F. Chop chicken and let cool. If eating now, add to the large bowl, add 2 tablespoons crunchy topping, and toss to combine. If eating later, divide chicken among the containers and secure lids. Refrigerate up to 1 week, then top and toss as directed.

2

SERVES 6
ACTIVE TIME: 20 MINUTES

PREP AHEAD

Shred kale and carrots

Slice bell peppers

Chop herbs

MAKE AHEAD

Refrigerate salads, without crunchy topping, up to 1 week

NOTES AND SHORTCUTS

Put your food processor to work to chop herbs, shred carrots, and even shred kale, once center ribs are removed

Whole Foods, Aldi, Safeway, and Sprouts carry grain-free french-fried onions; they contain buckwheat, which is not paleo but is gluten-free and grain-free, and are delicious on this salad

Save remaining dressing to use in future meal plans

Sub shrimp or salmon for chicken; eat within 3 days

Sub Primal Kitchen or SideDish brands for homemade dressing

Week 3

Chicken Parm Meatball Skillet 68

Chile-Garlic Chicken with Charred
Green Beans and Roasted Cashews 71

Orange-Sesame Chicken and Broccoli ✺ 72

Stuffed-Pepper Soup 75

Back-Pocket Dinner: Tuna Salad with Apples
and Pumpkin Seeds 238

3

This week's lineup capitalizes on shortcuts like frozen meatballs (either homemade or store-bought) and a jar of your favorite marinara sauce for the meatball skillet and doubling the Instant Pot sesame chicken and freezing a batch for later.

Batch Cookers and Freezer Preppers will be happy to know that all the meals can be prepped in advance; this means quick lunches, too. You could also make a double batch of the hearty soup to freeze for future enjoyment.

The make-ahead steps that follow assume you haven't already made the Ginger-Sesame Dressing (page 33) from last week or don't have any left (because it's *that* good!).

But if you *did* do menu plan 2 last week, chances are you still have some dressing left in the bottle and can skip making a new batch!

MAKE AHEAD

UP TO 1 WEEK
- Make meatballs (if using homemade)
- Make ginger-sesame dressing for chile-garlic chicken
- Make orange-sesame chicken and broccoli sauce

UP TO 3 DAYS
- Brown ground beef

UP TO 1 DAY
- Thaw meatballs in refrigerator

PREP AHEAD
- Chop parsley
- Trim green beans
- Chop bell peppers
- Chop green onions
- Mince 6 garlic cloves
- Dice yellow onion
- Slice red chiles

GROCERY LIST

PROTEIN

- Boneless, skinless chicken thighs 9 pounds
- Lean ground beef 2 pounds

PRODUCE

- Basil 1 bunch
- Fresh parsley 1 bunch
- Garlic cloves 14 (2 heads)
- Ginger 2-inch piece
- Green beans 12 ounces
- Green bell pepper 1
- Green onions 1 bunch
- Green salad for serving (optional)
- Large yellow onion 1
- Orange bell pepper 1
- Oranges 2
- Red bell pepper 1
- Red chiles 2

REFRIGERATOR

- Crumbled dairy-free feta cheese 1 cup
- Crumbled dairy-free mozzarella 1 cup
- Dairy-free grated Parmesan ¼ cup, plus more for serving

FREEZER

- Frozen broccoli florets 2 (10-ounce) packages
- Frozen cauliflower rice 2 (12-ounce) packages (1 package for serving)
- Frozen cooked chicken meatballs (see page 34) 2 pounds

CUPBOARD & COUNTER

- Arrowroot powder 3 tablespoons
- Cayenne pepper ¼ teaspoon
- Coconut aminos 1½ cups
- Coconut sugar 2 tablespoons
- Diced tomatoes 1 (26- to 28-ounce) can or jar
- Dry roasted cashews ⅓ cup
- Garlic powder 1 teaspoon
- Grain-free bread crumbs ⅓ cup
- Ground ginger 1½ teaspoons
- Italian seasoning 2½ teaspoons
- Honey 1 cup
- Marinara sauce 1 (24-ounce) jar
- Nutritional yeast 2 tablespoons
- Onion powder 1 teaspoon
- Red pepper flakes 2½ teaspoons
- Sesame seeds for garnishing
- Strained tomatoes 1 (24-ounce) bottle
- Tahini 2 tablespoons
- Toasted grain-free bread for dipping (optional)
- Toasted sesame oil ½ cup
- Tomato paste ⅓ cup
- Unsalted beef bone broth 32 ounces
- Unsalted chicken bone broth ½ cup
- Unseasoned rice vinegar ½ cup

3

Chicken Parm Meatball Skillet

SERVES 6
ACTIVE TIME: 22 MINUTES

MAKE AHEAD

Make meatballs up to
4 months

Refrigerate up to 5 days

Freeze up to 4 months

NOTES AND SHORTCUTS

Meatball brands: Amylu
Foods, Aidells, Trader Joe's

I use Miyoko's mozzarella;
sub shredded dairy
mozzarella, if desired

Sub smashed plantain chips,
almond flour, or pork rind
crumbs for bread crumbs

Sub sliced Italian sausages
for meatballs

2 tablespoons avocado oil

2 pounds frozen cooked chicken
meatballs (see page 34)

1 (24-ounce) jar marinara sauce

½ cup unsalted chicken
bone broth

⅓ cup grain-free bread crumbs

¼ cup dairy-free grated

Parmesan, plus more for serving

1 cup crumbled dairy-free
mozzarella

¼ cup chopped basil or
parsley leaves

Green salad for serving (optional)

Toasted grain-free bread
for dipping (optional)

In a medium heatproof skillet over medium heat, warm oil until it
shimmers. Add meatballs and brown on all sides, 3 to 5 minutes.
Then add marinara and broth, turn heat to medium-low, and let
simmer for 12 to 15 minutes, until meatballs are thawed and
heated through.

Meanwhile, in a small bowl, mix together bread crumbs and
Parmesan.

Sprinkle mozzarella over meatballs, then top with bread crumb
mixture.

Preheat broiler.

Transfer skillet to top rack under broiler and broil for 1 to 3 minutes,
until cheese is bubbling and golden brown. Sprinkle with basil.

Serve with green salad and toasted grain-free bread for dipping,
if desired.

Chile-Garlic Chicken with Charred Green Beans and Roasted Cashews

3 pounds boneless, skinless chicken thighs

Sea salt and cracked black pepper

1 tablespoon avocado oil

12 ounces trimmed green beans

1 orange bell pepper, seeded and chopped

½ cup Ginger-Sesame Dressing (page 33)

1 tablespoon arrowroot powder

½ teaspoon red pepper flakes

2 red chiles, seeds removed and thinly sliced

⅓ cup dry roasted cashews

1 bunch green onions, white and green parts. chopped

Season chicken thighs with salt and black pepper.

In a large skillet over medium-high heat, warm oil until it shimmers. Add chicken and pan-fry until cooked through, 4 to 6 minutes per side.

Using tongs, transfer chicken to a plate and pour off all but 1 tablespoon oil. Add green beans and bell pepper and sauté until browned and crisp-tender, 4 to 6 minutes.

In a small bowl, whisk together dressing and arrowroot powder and pour into pan. Turn heat to medium-high and bring to a boil for 2 to 3 minutes, until thickened and reduced to a syrup.

Return chicken to pan and simmer until reheated.

Serve hot, topped with red pepper flakes, chiles, cashews, and green onions.

3
___

SERVES 6
ACTIVE TIME: 22 MINUTES

PREP AHEAD

Trim green beans

Chop bell pepper

Seed and slice chiles

Chop green onions

___

MAKE AHEAD

Refrigerate dressing up to 2 weeks

Refrigerate chicken up to 1 week

Freeze chicken up to 4 months

___

NOTES AND SHORTCUTS

Sub ahi tuna steaks or mahi-mahi for chicken

3

PREP AHEAD

Mince garlic cloves

MAKE AHEAD

Refrigerate sauce
up to 3 weeks

Refrigerate, uncooked, up to
3 days; cooked, up to 1 week

Freeze, cooked, up to
4 months; uncooked,
6 months

NOTES AND SHORTCUTS

Sub your favorite stir-fry
sauce for coconut aminos,
sesame oil, and ginger

Orange-Sesame Chicken and Broccoli

1 cup coconut aminos

¾ cup honey

Zest of 1 orange, plus juice
of 2 oranges

⅓ cup tomato paste

3 tablespoons toasted sesame oil

6 garlic cloves, minced

1½ teaspoons ground ginger

1½ teaspoons red pepper flakes

2¼ teaspoons sea salt

1 teaspoon cracked black pepper

6 pounds boneless, skinless
chicken thighs

2 tablespoons arrowroot powder

2 (10-ounce) packages frozen
broccoli florets

Cauliflower rice for serving

Sesame seeds and chopped green
onions for garnishing

Make one batch to cook now and a second batch to freeze for later.

In a medium bowl, whisk together coconut aminos, honey, orange
zest and juice, tomato paste, oil, garlic, ginger, red pepper flakes,
salt, and black pepper into a sauce.

Equally divide chicken thighs between your cooking pot (Instant
Pot or slow cooker) and a 9-inch glass container or freezer bag.
Pour half of sauce into each container. Seal one container and
store in freezer for later.

TO COOK NOW

Instant Pot: Secure lid and set valve to seal. Cook chicken and sauce
on manual high heat with a 10-minute timer. Quick-release pressure.
Spoon fat off top of sauce, then turn machine to sauté mode high.

In a small bowl, whisk together 1 tablespoon arrowroot powder and
2 tablespoons juices from pot into a slurry. Stir slurry into pot, add
1 package frozen broccoli, and let simmer for 5 to 10 minutes, until
sauce is thickened.

Slow Cooker: Cook chicken and sauce on low for 6 hours or high for
3 hours.

In a small bowl, whisk together 1 tablespoon arrowroot powder and
2 tablespoons juices from pot to make a slurry. Stir slurry into pot
and add 1 package frozen broccoli. Cook on high heat, uncovered,
for 20 minutes, until broccoli is crisp-tender and sauce is thickened.

Using two forks, coarsely shred chicken in pot. Serve hot, over
cauliflower rice, garnished with a sprinkle of sesame seeds and
green onions.

TO COOK LATER

Remove container from freezer.

Instant Pot: Once thawed just enough to remove contents, cook as directed above but use a 30-minute timer.

Slow Cooker: Once thawed completely, cook as directed.

Stuffed-Pepper Soup

2 pounds lean ground beef

1 green bell pepper, seeded and chopped

1 red bell pepper, seeded and chopped

1 large yellow onion, diced

1 (26- to 28-ounce) can or jar diced tomatoes

1 (24-ounce) bottle strained tomatoes

32 ounces unsalted beef bone broth

¼ cup chopped parsley, plus more for garnishing

2 tablespoons coconut sugar

2 tablespoons nutritional yeast

2½ teaspoons Italian seasoning

1 tablespoon sea salt

1 teaspoon garlic powder

1 teaspoon onion powder

½ teaspoon cracked black pepper

½ teaspoon red pepper flakes

1 (12-ounce) package frozen cauliflower rice

1 cup crumbled dairy-free feta cheese

SERVES 6 TO 8
ACTIVE TIME: 35 MINUTES

PREP AHEAD

Chop bell pepper

Dice onion

MAKE AHEAD

Refrigerate up to 1 week

Freeze up to 6 months

NOTES AND SHORTCUTS

Sub ground turkey for beef

Sub 1 teaspoon each basil and oregano for Italian seasoning

Sub 1 tablespoon honey for coconut sugar

Sub 1 cup grated Parmesan for nutritional yeast

Violife and Trader Joe's offer dairy-free feta. Sub grated Pecorino Romano or mozzarella

Sub 2 cups undercooked white rice for cauliflower rice

Stovetop: In a large Dutch oven over medium-high heat, brown ground beef for 7 to 10 minutes. Stir in both bell peppers, onion, diced tomatoes, strained tomatoes, broth, parsley, coconut sugar, nutritional yeast, Italian seasoning, salt, garlic powder, onion powder, black pepper, and red pepper flakes. Turn heat to low and let simmer for 10 minutes.

Stir cauliflower rice into beef and continue to simmer for 10 to 12 minutes, until rice is tender.

Slow Cooker: Brown beef on stovetop and transfer to a slow cooker. Add all ingredients, except feta and parsley for garnish, and cook on low for 8 hours or on high for 4 hours.

Serve hot, garnished with feta cheese and parsley.

Week 4

4

This week's menu is all about making the most of your time, starting with the chicken salad, which gets an easy upgrade with precooked chicken. If you are following these plans chronologically, this is your first introduction to my magic sauce—the zesty, tangy green goddess dressing, which is packed with fiber from being infused with tons of herbs. This week we use it on the salmon, but you will see it quite a few more times because I'm obsessed with how it brings every salad and dinner to life.

Simplify your kitchen tasks by using a food processor to chop the celery, garlic, and green onions (store each separately).

Aside from the salmon, which is best eaten within two days, every meal can be prepped ahead, making this week a breeze for those who love to batch-cook. Consider doubling stir-fry and egg roll bowls for freezer-friendly convenience; your future self will thank you for it. You can add any leftover herbs to the green goddess dressing and make it extra herby, or, if you choose, sprinkle whatever is left in your jar to liven it up.

MAKE AHEAD

UP TO 1 WEEK
- Make green goddess dressing for salmon
- Make stir-fry sauce for sweet and spicy chicken
- Make firecracker sauce for sweet and spicy chicken

UP TO 3 DAYS
- Make cranberry–poppy seed dressing for chicken salad
- Cut and toss chicken in arrowroot

UP TO 1 DAY
- Season and "bread" salmon

PREP AHEAD
- Chop rotisserie chicken
- Thinly slice celery
- Chop walnuts
- Halve potatoes
- Mix bread crumb mixture
- Trim broccolini ends
- Wash and dry herbs
- Mince garlic cloves
- Chop 2 green onions
- Cut and coat chicken breasts
- Slice bok choy
- Chop bell pepper
- Slice green onions

GROCERY LIST

PROTEIN

- Ground pork 3 pounds
- Rotisserie dark and white meat chicken 2 whole chickens
- Skinless, boneless chicken breasts 1½ pounds
- Wild-caught salmon 4 (4- to 6-ounce) fillets

PRODUCE

- Baby arugula ½ cup
- Baby bok choy 2 heads
- Baby potatoes 1 pound
- Broccolini 2 bunches
- Celery stalks 6
- Chives 1 small bunch
- Coleslaw mix 1 (12-ounce) package
- Fresh mixed fresh herbs, such as dill, tarragon, parsley, basil, or mint (packed) 2 bunches of your choice
- Fresh snow peas 1 (6-ounce) package
- Garlic cloves 5
- Green onions 2 bunches
- Lemons 3
- Red bell pepper 1

REFRIGERATOR

- Soft dairy-free goat cheese 4 ounces
- Unsweetened cashew milk ¾ cup

CUPBOARD & COUNTER

- Apple cider vinegar 3 teaspoons
- Apple juice–sweetened dried cranberries ½ cup
- Arrowroot powder ¼ cup
- Avocado oil mayonnaise ⅔ cup
- Coconut aminos 2 cups
- Fish sauce 2 tablespoons plus 2 teaspoons
- Full-fat coconut milk ⅓ cup
- Garlic powder ¾ teaspoon
- Grain-free bread crumbs ¼ cup
- Grain-free crackers or toasted slices grain-free bread for serving
- Grain-free french-fried onions for serving (optional)
- Ground ginger ¾ teaspoon
- Healthy in a Hurry Cajun Seasoning (page 37) 1½ teaspoons
- Honey ⅓ cup
- Poppy seeds 1½ tablespoons
- Red pepper flakes ½ teaspoon
- Sriracha ½ cup
- Sriracha aioli for serving (optional)
- Toasted sesame oil 2 tablespoons plus 2 teaspoons
- Unseasoned rice vinegar 1 tablespoon
- Walnut pieces 1½ cups
- White pepper 1 teaspoon

4

PREP AHEAD

Chop chicken

Thinly slice celery

Chop walnuts

MAKE AHEAD

Refrigerate up to 5 days

NOTES AND SHORTCUTS

Sub leftover turkey for rotisserie chicken

Sub canned chicken for rotisserie chicken

Sub pecans for walnuts

Cranberry-Poppy Seed Chicken Salad

⅔ cup avocado-oil mayonnaise

⅓ cup full-fat coconut milk

1½ tablespoons fresh lemon juice

1½ tablespoons poppy seeds

½ teaspoon sea salt

½ teaspoon cracked black pepper

6 cups rotisserie dark and white meat chicken, chopped

6 celery stalks, thinly sliced

1½ cups walnut pieces, chopped

½ cup apple juice–sweetened dried cranberries

Grain-free crackers or toasted slices grain-free bread for serving

In a medium bowl, whisk together mayonnaise, coconut milk, lemon juice, poppy seeds, salt, and black pepper. Stir in chicken, celery, walnuts, and cranberries.

Serve immediately with grain-free crackers or between two slices of grain-free bread.

Crispy Green Goddess Salmon with Broccolini, Potatoes, and Arugula

1 pound baby potatoes, halved

3 tablespoons avocado oil

Sea salt and cracked black pepper

¼ cup grain-free bread crumbs

1½ teaspoons Healthy in a Hurry Cajun Seasoning (page 37)

2 bunches broccolini, trimmed

4 (4- to 6-ounce) wild-caught salmon fillets

GREEN GODDESS DRESSING

4-ounces soft dairy-free goat cheese

¾ cup unsweetened cashew milk

¼ cup extra-virgin olive oil

Zest and juice of 1 lemon

2 garlic cloves

1½ cups packed mixed fresh herbs, such as dill, tarragon, parsley, basil, or mint

1 small bunch chives

1½ teaspoons sea salt

¼ teaspoon cracked black pepper

½ cup baby arugula

Lemon wedges for serving

Preheat oven to 425°F. Line a baking sheet with parchment paper.

Place potatoes on prepared baking sheet and toss with 1 tablespoon oil, then season with salt and black pepper. Bake for 20 minutes, or until tender.

While potatoes are cooking, in a shallow bowl, combine remaining 2 tablespoons avocado oil, bread crumbs, Cajun seasoning, and a pinch each salt and black pepper.

Remove potatoes from oven, add broccolini, and push to one side of pan. Add salmon on other side and rub bread crumb mixture on tops. Return pan to oven and bake for 10 to 15 minutes, until salmon begins to flake in center.

To make dressing: While salmon cooks, in a blender or using a jar and immersion blender, blend goat cheese, cashew milk, olive oil, lemon zest and juice, garlic, herbs, chives, salt, and black pepper until smooth and creamy.

Serve hot with a drizzle of sauce and baby arugula sprinkled over top. Serve lemon wedges alongside.

PREP AHEAD

Halve potatoes

Mix bread crumb mixture

Trim broccolini ends

MAKE AHEAD

Refrigerate sauce up to 2 weeks

Refrigerate salmon up to 2 days

NOTES AND SHORTCUTS

Sub smashed plantain chips, almond flour, or pork rind crumbs for bread crumbs

Goat cheese brands: Treeline and Spero make dairy-free goat cheese; if dairy is tolerated, select a soft, spreadable goat cheese

Sub coconut milk for cashew milk

Sub dairy-free ricotta for goat cheese

Sub peeled and cubed parsnips for potatoes

Sub watercress or herb sprigs for arugula

Sub bone-in, skin-on chicken thighs for salmon and cook with potatoes and broccolini, 30 to 35 minutes.

4

PREP AHEAD

Mince garlic

Chop green onions

MAKE AHEAD

Refrigerate stir-fry sauce up to 1 month

Refrigerate bowls up to 1 week

Freeze bowls up to 4 months

NOTES AND SHORTCUTS

Whole Foods, Aldi, Safeway, and Sprouts carry grain-free french-fried onions; they contain buckwheat, which is not paleo but is gluten-free and grain-free. Adding them is optional, but they taste and give a crunch of a traditional egg-roll wrapper.

Substitute ground chicken for pork

In place of sriracha aioli, use any spicy mayonnaise or mix together ½ cup mayonnaise, 2 tablespoons sriracha, juice of 1 lime, 1 teaspoon sea salt, and ¾ teaspoon cayenne pepper; refrigerate up to 1 month

Egg Roll Bowls

1 tablespoon avocado oil

3 garlic cloves, minced

1 bunch green onions, trimmed, white parts chopped, and tender green parts chopped and reserved

3 pounds ground pork

1 (12-ounce) package coleslaw mix

½ cup Stir-Fry Sauce (page 186)

Sriracha aioli and grain-free french-fried onions for serving (optional)

In a large skillet over medium heat, warm oil until it shimmers. Add garlic and white parts of green onions and sauté for 3 to 5 minutes, until fragrant and garlic is golden. Add ground pork and turn heat to medium-high. Sauté, breaking up pork with a wooden spoon, until cooked through, 6 to 8 minutes. Stir in coleslaw mix and stir-fry sauce and bring to a boil. Turn heat to medium-low and let simmer for 5 minutes, until slaw mix is tender and liquid has absorbed into meat.

Serve hot, with green parts of scallions sprinkled on top. If desired, drizzle with sriracha aioli and sprinkle with french-fried onions.

Sweet and Spicy Chicken Stir-Fry

1½ pounds boneless, skinless chicken breasts, cut into 1-inch chunks

¼ cup arrowroot powder

4 tablespoons avocado oil

2 heads baby bok choy, thinly sliced

1 red bell pepper, seeded and cubed

1 bunch green onions, trimmed and thinly sliced, white and green parts separated

FIRECRACKER SAUCE

½ cup sriracha

⅓ cup honey

3 teaspoons apple cider vinegar

1½ teaspoons sea salt

¾ teaspoon ground ginger

¾ teaspoon garlic powder

½ teaspoon red pepper flakes

1 (6-ounce) package fresh snow peas

SERVES 4
ACTIVE TIME: 40 MINUTES

PREP AHEAD

Cut and coat chicken breasts

Slice bok choy

Cube bell pepper

Slice green onions

Prepare sauce

MAKE AHEAD

Refrigerate sauce up to 1 month

Refrigerate meal up to 1 week

Freeze up to 3 months

NOTES AND SHORTCUTS

Sriracha brands: Sprouts, True Made Foods, Yellowbird, Natural Value, and Fix

Sub buffalo sauce such as Frank's RedHot Original for sriracha

Sub ketchup for sriracha and omit red pepper flakes for milder version

Sub shrimp for chicken; cook until pink

Sub broccoli for bok choy

In a medium bowl, toss together chicken and arrowroot powder, ensuring pieces are well coated. Set aside.

In a large skillet over medium-high heat, warm 1 tablespoon oil until it shimmers. Add bok choy, bell pepper, and white parts of green onions and stir-fry for 2 to 3 minutes, until crisp-tender. Remove vegetables from skillet and set aside.

Line a large plate with paper towels.

Add remaining 3 tablespoons oil to skillet and warm over medium-high heat until it shimmers. Working in batches, add chicken and pan-fry until browned on all sides, 3 to 5 minutes. Transfer to prepared plate to drain.

To make sauce: In a small bowl, whisk together sriracha, honey, vinegar, salt, ginger, garlic powder, and red pepper flakes.

Once all chicken has been cooked, discard oil in skillet. Add sauce to skillet over medium-high heat and bring mixture to a boil, scraping to incorporate any bits from pan. Add vegetables, chicken, and snow peas and gently stir to coat. Top with green parts of green onions.

Serve hot.

Week 5

Buffalo Chicken Sheet-Pan Pasta 92

Sausage and Fennel Linguine 95

Enchilada-Stuffed Sweet Potatoes 96

Cali Salmon Bowls 99

Back-Pocket Dinner:
Baked Pesto Gnocchi and Sausage 245

5

This week's plan is full of one-pan wonders and easy dinners that rely on an exciting array of flavor-elevating sauces. There is no lack of punch in these meals.

Prepare the sauces from scratch at the start of the week by tapping into your Component Prepper persona. They can be stored for weeks, ready to serve as building blocks for future quick and delicious meals.

If convenience is your goal, I've also provided store-bought shortcuts that preserve the bold flavors without sacrificing precious time. The sweet potatoes work well with any ground meat (beef, turkey, bison, chicken)—so grab whatever you have in your freezer and use it up.

Embrace the art of preparation by prepping the make-ahead components that follow. Roast the sweet potatoes for a hassle-free addition to your meals. And don't forget that spaghetti squash reheats beautifully, and it perfectly complements the buffalo chicken.

MAKE AHEAD

UP TO 1 WEEK

- Spiral-slice noodles for linguine
- Make sauce for linguine
- Scrub and cook sweet potatoes
- Make red enchilada sauce for stuffed sweet potatoes
- Make tahini dressing for Cali bowls

UP TO 5 DAYS

- Soften the skin and slice spaghetti squash for buffalo chicken
- Make enchilada filling

UP TO 3 DAYS

- Toss cauliflower in oil and seasonings

UP TO 1 DAY

- Season salmon

PREP AHEAD

- Slice carrots and celery
- Spiral-slice parsnips
- Mince garlic and onion
- Slice fennel bulb
- Dice onion and poblano peppers
- Break cauliflower into florets
- Slice cucumbers and radishes

GROCERY LIST

PROTEIN

- Boneless, skinless chicken breasts 2 pounds
- Ground meat (chicken, bison, beef, or turkey) 2 pounds
- Mild Italian sausage 1 pound
- Skin-on salmon 4 (6-ounce) fillets

PRODUCE

- Avocados 2, plus more to garnish Enchilada-Stuffed Sweet Potatoes (optional)
- Cauliflower 1 head
- Celery for serving
- Cilantro 1 bunch
- Fennel 1 bulb
- Fresh lemon juice 2 tablespoons
- Garlic cloves 10
- Green onions 1 bunch
- Lacinato kale 1 small bunch
- Medium parsnips 3
- Medium poblano chiles 2
- Medium sweet potatoes 6
- Parsley for serving
- Persian cucumbers 2
- Radishes 1 bunch
- Shredded lettuce for topping (optional)
- Sliced black olives for topping (optional)
- Sliced carrots for serving
- Spaghetti squash 1 (3-pound)
- Yellow onions 2

REFRIGERATOR

- Dairy-free pesto ¼ cup
- Dairy-free ranch dressing ¼ cup plus more for serving
- Dairy-free sour cream for topping (optional)
- Pickled onions 1 cup

CUPBOARD & COUNTER

- Arrowroot powder 3 tablespoons
- Buffalo wing sauce ¼ cup
- Ghee 3 tablespoons
- Ground cumin ¼ teaspoon
- Healthy in a Hurry Taco Seasoning (page 37) 3½ tablespoons
- Maple syrup 2 tablespoons
- Mild ground curry powder ¾ teaspoon
- Red pepper flakes ½ teaspoon
- Red wine vinegar 1 teaspoon
- Strained tomatoes 1 (24-ounce) bottle
- Tahini ½ cup
- Toasted pepitas for garnishing
- Tomato paste 7 ounces
- Unsalted chicken bone broth 2½ cups

5

SERVES 6
ACTIVE TIME: 45 MINUTES

PREP AHEAD

Soften the skin and slice
spaghetti squash

Refrigerate ranch dressing
up to 1 month

Slice carrots and celery

MAKE AHEAD

Refrigerate up to 1 week

NOTES AND SHORTCUTS

Sub store-bought ranch
dressing, such as Tessemae's
or Primal Kitchen

Primal Kitchen buffalo
sauce is one of my favorites

Buffalo Chicken Sheet-Pan Pasta

1 (3-pound) spaghetti squash

2 pounds boneless, skinless
chicken breasts

2 tablespoons avocado oil

¾ teaspoon sea salt

¼ teaspoon cracked black pepper

¼ cup Dairy-Free Ranch Dressing
(page 32), plus more for serving

¼ cup buffalo sauce

Parsley and sliced celery and
carrots for serving

Place squash directly on middle rack of oven and turn temperature
to 400°F. Once oven preheat timer goes off (about 10 minutes),
carefully remove squash. This will soften squash enough to slice it.

Meanwhile, line a half sheet pan with parchment paper.

Arrange chicken in a single layer on prepared pan. Drizzle with
1 tablespoon oil and sprinkle with salt and black pepper.

Once squash has cooled enough to handle, slice off both ends
and cut crosswise into four or five rounds. Scoop out seeds from
center of each round. Drizzle both sides of rounds with remaining
1 tablespoon oil and season with salt and black pepper. Arrange
in a single layer on prepared pan.

Place pan on middle rack of oven and bake for 20 to 25 minutes,
until chicken is cooked through and squash is fork-tender. Dice
chicken and return it to one side of pan.

Using a fork, pull flesh from sides of squash rounds into noodle-like
strands. Heap noodles onto other side of pan; discard skins.

Drizzle ranch dressing on top of noodles and toss to mix. Toss
chicken in buffalo sauce.

Serve chicken over squash noodles along with parsley, celery, and
carrots. Pass additional ranch alongside.

Sausage and Fennel Linguine

1 pound mild Italian sausage, casings removed and crumbled

4 garlic cloves, minced

1 fennel bulb, thinly sliced, fronds reserved

1 yellow onion, diced

½ teaspoon red pepper flakes

3 medium parsnips

1 (24-ounce) bottle strained tomatoes

½ cup unsalted chicken bone broth

1 teaspoon red wine vinegar

1 teaspoon sea salt

½ teaspoon cracked black pepper

1 small bunch lacinato kale, ribs removed

SERVES 4 TO 6
ACTIVE TIME: 25 MINUTES

PREP AHEAD

Spiral-slice parsnips

Mince garlic and onion

Slice fennel bulb

MAKE AHEAD

Refrigerate sauce up to 1 week

Refrigerate noodles in cold water up to 1 week

Freeze sauce up to 6 months

NOTES AND SHORTCUTS

No spiralizer? Use a vegetable peeler to shave parsnips into thick strips or a julienne vegetable peeler to slice into thin strips

Sub 8 cups roasted cauliflower florets for parsnip noodles

Sub 1 pound cooked al dente grain-free pasta, such as cassava or chickpea, for parsnip noodles

In a Dutch oven over medium-high heat, brown sausage. Add garlic, sliced fennel, onion, and red pepper flakes and sauté for 5 to 7 minutes, until fennel is tender. Set aside.

While sausage mixture sautés, using a vegetable spiralizer, cut parsnips into linguine-size noodles.

Fill a large pot with salted water and bring to a boil. Add parsnip noodles and cook for 2 minutes, until crisp-tender but still holding their shape. Drain and set aside.

Add tomatoes, broth, and vinegar to Dutch oven and season with salt and black pepper. Return pot to stovetop, turn heat to low, and bring to a simmer.

Chop kale and fennel fronds.

Add noodles to sauce, remove pan from heat, and stir in kale and fennel fronds.

Serve hot.

5

SERVES 6

ACTIVE TIME: 55 MINUTES

PREP AHEAD

Scrub and cook sweet potatoes

Dice onion and poblano peppers

MAKE AHEAD

Refrigerate enchilada sauce up to 1 month; freeze up to 6 months

Refrigerate cooked sweet potatoes and filling up to 5 days

Freeze filling up to 4 months

NOTES AND SHORTCUTS

Enchilada sauce brands: Siete and Sprouts

Use any grain-free taco seasoning; check for rice starch or other anti-caking agents

To cook sweet potatoes in an Instant Pot: Pour 1 cup water into cooker, add a steamer insert, and place sweet potatoes on insert. Secure lid, set valve to seal. Cook on high pressure with a 15-minute timer. Quick-release pressure.

Sub leftover shredded beef (see page 156) or shredded rotisserie chicken for ground meat

Enchilada-Stuffed Sweet Potatoes

6 medium sweet potatoes, scrubbed clean

1 tablespoon avocado oil

1 teaspoon coarse sea salt

FILLING

2 tablespoons avocado oil

1 yellow onion, diced

2 medium poblano chiles, seeds removed and diced

4 garlic cloves, minced

1½ teaspoons sea salt

2 pounds ground meat (chicken, bison, beef, or turkey)

RED ENCHILADA SAUCE

3 tablespoons ghee

3 tablespoons arrowroot powder

3½ tablespoons Healthy in a Hurry Taco Seasoning (page 37)

7 ounces tomato paste

2 cups unsalted chicken bone broth

Dairy-free sour cream, sliced avocado, cilantro, sliced black olives, and shredded lettuce for topping (optional)

Preheat oven to 400°F. Line a baking sheet with parchment paper or aluminum foil.

Rub skins of sweet potatoes all over with oil and pat with coarse salt. Using a fork, prick skins a few times and place on prepared baking sheet. Bake until tender, about 40 minutes.

To make filling: While potatoes are baking, in a large skillet over medium-high heat, warm oil until it shimmers. Add onion, poblanos, garlic, and sea salt and sauté for 5 minutes. Add ground meat and continue cooking until meat is cooked through and vegetables are softened, about 10 minutes.

To make sauce: While filling is cooking, in a medium saucepan over medium heat, melt ghee. Whisk in arrowroot powder and cook for 2 minutes. Add taco seasoning and stir for 2 minutes longer, until fragrant. Add tomato paste and broth and whisk until smooth. Turn heat to low and let simmer for 5 minutes to thicken. (Let cool completely before storing.)

Cut slits in tops of cooked sweet potatoes and open them up a bit. Spoon ⅓ cup filling into each and top with 2 to 3 tablespoons sauce.

Serve with sour cream, avocado, cilantro, olives, and lettuce, if desired.

Cali Salmon Bowls

1 head cauliflower,
broken into florets

2 tablespoons avocado oil

1¼ teaspoons fine sea salt

¾ teaspoon mild ground
curry powder

4 (6-ounce) skin-on salmon fillets

½ teaspoon cracked black pepper

TAHINI DRESSING

½ cup tahini

2 tablespoons fresh lemon juice

2 tablespoons maple syrup

2 garlic cloves, minced

½ teaspoon sea salt

¼ teaspoon ground cumin

2 Persian cucumbers, sliced

1 bunch radishes, thinly sliced

1 cup pickled onions

2 avocados, halved and sliced

¼ cup dairy-free pesto (page 32)

Chopped green onions or
cilantro leaves and toasted
pepitas for garnishing

SERVES 4 TO 6
ACTIVE TIME: 28 MINUTES

PREP AHEAD

Break cauliflower
into florets

Slice cucumbers and
radishes

MAKE AHEAD

Refrigerate dressing
up to 4 weeks

Refrigerate roasted
cauliflower up to 1 week

Refrigerate composed
bowls up to 3 days

NOTES AND SHORTCUTS

Purchase fresh dairy-
free pesto (I prefer a
refrigerated one over a
shelf-stable one) or make
your own

Preheat oven to 400°F. Line a half sheet pan with parchment paper.

Pile cauliflower on prepared sheet pan, top with 1 tablespoon oil, ¾ teaspoon salt, and curry powder and toss to coat. Spread florets in a single layer and roast for 5 minutes.

Meanwhile, rub salmon fillets with remaining 1 tablespoon oil, remaining ½ teaspoon salt, and black pepper.

Remove pan from oven and push cauliflower to edges of pan. Place salmon fillets, skin-side down, along center of pan. Return pan to oven and roast for 6 to 8 minutes, until salmon flakes slightly in center.

Make the dressing: While the salmon cooks, in a small bowl, whisk together tahini, lemon juice, maple syrup, garlic, sea salt, and cumin. Thin with a little water, if needed.

Divide salmon and cauliflower equally among serving bowls. Top with cucumbers, radishes, pickled onions, and avocado slices. Spoon pesto over salmon and cauliflower, then drizzle about 1 tablespoon dressing over each bowl. Garnish with green onions and pepitas.

Serve warm.

Week 6

6

This week, invest just 10 minutes up front to effortlessly prepare a tender pork roast in an Instant Pot or slow cooker, and you will have set the stage for a week of no-fuss meals. From this foundation comes two fantastic and flavorful dishes: a Cuban-inspired sheet-pan quesadilla bake and a vegetable-rich fried rice with pineapple that's coated in a delectable soy- and sugar-free teriyaki sauce.

To round out the menu with something refreshing and light, there's a grilled salmon salad with zesty citrus dressing and snappy peas, along with my reliable chicken bowls, featuring an avocado dressing. With freezer-ready ground chicken as a backup, convenience and flavor go hand in hand. My family loves these bowls with ground chicken, so I always get a few pounds when it's on sale at Trader Joe's or ButcherBox and keep it in the freezer for this last-minute dinner.

MAKE AHEAD

UP TO 1 WEEK
- Make carnitas
- Make sauce for quesadillas
- Make dressing for salmon salad

UP TO 5 DAYS
- Cook chicken for southwestern bowls

UP TO 3 DAYS
- Make avocado ranch dressing for southwestern bowls

UP TO 1 DAY
- Marinate salmon
- Toast hemp hearts and sesame seeds for salmon salad

PREP AHEAD
- Shred pork
- Mince 5 garlic cloves
- Dice 3 bell peppers
- Chop green onions
- Dice pineapple
- Peel and cut oranges
- Cut 2 cucumbers into matchsticks
- Thinly slice snap peas
- Wash and dry kale
- Wash and shred romaine
- Grate jicama
- Halve tomatoes

GROCERY LIST

PROTEIN

- Deli-style honey ham 6 slices
- Ground chicken 2 pounds
- Shredded pork 3½ cups
- Skinless, boneless pork shoulder (Boston butt) 5 pounds
- Wild-caught salmon 1½ pounds

PRODUCE

- Arugula for serving
- Avocados 4
- Baby kale 6 cups
- Cherry tomatoes 1 pint
- Cilantro 1 bunch
- Green bell pepper 1
- Green onions 1 small bunch
- Jalapeños 3, for mild
- Jicama 1
- Large garlic cloves 5
- Lime 1
- Orange bell pepper 1
- Oranges 3
- Persian cucumbers 2
- Pineapple 1
- Red bell pepper 1
- Romaine lettuce 2 heads
- Sugar snap peas 8 ounces

REFRIGERATOR

- Crumbled dairy-free cheese ½ cup (optional)
- Dairy-free ranch dressing ½ cup
- Dill pickle sandwich slices 12
- Eggs 2
- Fresh orange juice 1⅔ cups
- Grain-free tortillas 12
- Mayonnaise ⅓ cup

FREEZER

- Frozen cauliflower rice 2 (12-ounce) packages

CUPBOARD & COUNTER

- Dijon mustard 3 tablespoons
- Dried oregano ¼ teaspoon
- Ghee 3 tablespoons
- Grain-free tortilla chips 1 bag
- Ground cumin ½ teaspoon
- Healthy in a Hurry Adobo Seasoning (page 36) 3 tablespoons
- Healthy in a Hurry Taco Seasoning (page 37) 1½ tablespoons
- Hemp hearts (hulled hemp seeds) 2 tablespoons
- Potato chips for serving
- Sesame seeds 1 tablespoon
- Teriyaki sauce ⅓ cup
- Tomato paste 1 tablespoon

6

SERVES 8 TO 10
ACTIVE TIME: 10 MINUTES
(PLUS 45 MINUTES PRESSURE
COOKING TIME)

PREP AHEAD

Cut, stem, and seed
jalapeños

MAKE AHEAD

Refrigerate up to 1 week

Freeze up to 4 months

NOTES AND SHORTCUTS

Sub 1 teaspoon each
oregano, pepper, coriander,
and cumin for adobo

Prep Recipe: Shredded Carnitas Pork

5 pounds boneless, skinless pork shoulder (Boston butt), cut into 4-inch chunks

3 jalapeños, cut in half lengthwise, stemmed, and seeded for mild

5 large garlic cloves

2½ teaspoons sea salt

1½ cups fresh orange juice

3 tablespoons Healthy in a Hurry Adobo Seasoning (page 36)

In a 6-quart Instant Pot, combine pork, jalapeños, garlic, salt, orange juice, and adobo seasoning and rub pork all over. Secure lid and set valve to seal. Cook on high pressure with a 45-minute timer. Let pressure release naturally.

Alternatively, in a slow cooker, combine pork, jalapeños, garlic, salt, orange juice, and adobo seasoning and rub pork all over. Cook on low heat for 8 hours.

Using an electric handheld mixer or two forks, shred pork directly in pot.

Transfer half the pork to a 9-inch glass container or freezer bag. Seal and store in the refrigerator to use later this week. Transfer the remaining pork, in 2-cup portions (for easy removal to use in other recipes), to glass containers or freezer bags and seal and store in the freezer for later.

Fried Pineapple and Pork Rice

2 tablespoons extra-virgin olive oil

2 cups shredded pork (see page 104)

1 tablespoon avocado oil

1 red bell pepper, seeded and diced

1 green bell pepper, seeded and diced

1 small bunch green onions, trimmed and chopped, white and green parts separated

2 (12-ounce) packages frozen cauliflower rice

2 cups diced pineapple

2 eggs, beaten

⅓ cup teriyaki sauce

Preheat broiler. Brush a quarter sheet pan with olive oil.

Spread pork evenly over bottom of prepared pan and place in oven on top rack for 5 to 7 minutes to crisp.

Meanwhile, in a large skillet over medium-high, warm avocado oil until it shimmers. Add both bell peppers and white parts of green onions and sauté for 5 to 7 minutes, until onions are soft.

Add cauliflower rice and pineapple to skillet and sauté for 3 to 5 minutes longer, until cauliflower is tender. Push vegetables to side of skillet, add eggs in open spot, and scramble. Stir gently to incorporate eggs. Stir in crisped pork and drizzle with sauce. Sprinkle with green parts of green onions.

Serve hot.

SERVES 4 TO 6
ACTIVE TIME: 30 MINUTES

PREP AHEAD

Dice red and green bell peppers

Chop green onions

Dice pineapple

Beat eggs

MAKE AHEAD

Refrigerate up to 1 week; freeze in 2-cup portions (for easy removal to use in other recipes) up to 4 months

Refrigerate fried rice up to 1 week; freeze up to 4 months

NOTES AND SHORTCUTS

Soy-free teriyaki brands: Thrive Market, Primal Kitchen, Coconut Secret, Kevin's Natural Foods

Sub shredded rotisserie chicken or shrimp for pork

6

SERVES 6
ACTIVE TIME: 25 MINUTES

PREP AHEAD

Refrigerate mayonnaise sauce up to 2 weeks

MAKE AHEAD

Refrigerate quesadillas up to 5 days

Freeze quesadillas, individually wrapped, up to 4 months

Reheat in toaster oven at 400°F, in a dry skillet over medium heat, or in an air fryer

NOTES AND SHORTCUTS

Grain-free tortilla brands: Onana Foods plantain tortillas, Siete almond flour tortillas, and Thrive Market coconut wraps

Cook quesadillas all at once on an electric griddle over medium heat in place of sheet pan

Sub cooked bacon or prosciutto for ham

Sub avocado oil for ghee

Whisk together 2 tablespoons aioli and 3 tablespoons olive oil for a simple salad dressing.

If cheese is tolerated, ½ cup shredded sheep's milk cheese, such as Manchego or Lamb Chopper by Cypress Grove, is amazing melted on these

Cuban Pork Sheet-Pan Quesadillas

3 tablespoons melted ghee

1½ cups shredded pork (see page 104)

⅓ cup mayonnaise

2 tablespoons Dijon mustard

2 tablespoons fresh orange juice

½ teaspoon ground cumin

¼ teaspoon dried oregano

12 grain-free tortillas

6 slices deli-style honey ham

12 dill pickle sandwich slices

½ cup crumbled dairy-free cheese (optional)

Potato chips and arugula salad for serving

Preheat oven to 400°F. Line a half sheet pan with parchment paper and brush with 1½ tablespoons ghee.

In a saucepan over medium-high heat, reheat pork in its juices.

While pork reheats, whisk together mayonnaise, mustard, orange juice, cumin, and oregano into a sauce.

Drain juices from pork.

Arrange six tortillas on prepared pan, overlapping them slightly. Spread tortillas with 1½ tablespoons mayonnaise sauce, then top with ham, pork, pickle slices, and cheese (if using). Top with six remaining tortillas, overlapping in same fashion. Brush tops of tortillas with remaining 1½ tablespoons ghee.

Place pan in oven on top rack and bake for 8 to 12 minutes. Slice quesadillas into rectangles.

Serve with potato chips and an arugula salad.

Citrus Salmon with Orange-Cucumber Salad

Zest and juice of 1 small orange, plus 2 large oranges

1 tablespoon Dijon mustard

½ cup avocado oil

Sea salt and cracked black pepper

1½ pounds wild-caught salmon

2 tablespoons hemp hearts (hulled hemp seeds)

1 tablespoon sesame seeds

6 cups baby kale

2 Persian cucumbers, cut into matchsticks

8 ounces sugar snap peas, trimmed and thinly sliced

1 avocado, thinly sliced

PREP AHEAD

Make dressing

Marinate salmon

Toast hemp hearts and sesame seeds

Wash and dry kale

Prepare oranges, cucumbers, and snap peas

MAKE AHEAD

Refrigerate salad, salmon separately, up to 3 days

NOTES AND SHORTCUTS

Sub skinless chicken thighs or ahi tuna steaks for salmon

Sub baby spinach for kale

In a small bowl, whisk together orange zest and juice and mustard. Slowly drizzle in oil, whisking continuously into a dressing. Season with a generous pinch of salt and black pepper.

Place salmon in a large shallow dish, pour in ¼ cup dressing, and let marinate for 30 minutes at room temperature.

In a small dry skillet over medium heat, combine hemp hearts, sesame seeds, and a pinch of salt and toast for 2 to 3 minutes.

Carefully cut away peel and pith of oranges and slice them into rounds.

In a large bowl, massage kale with remaining dressing. Add oranges, cucumbers, and snap peas. Set salad aside.

Prepare a grill for medium-high heat. Grill salmon for 3 to 4 minutes per side for medium-rare, more or less time depending on your desired degree of doneness.

Flake salmon and place on top of salad. Sprinkle with toasted hemp hearts and sesame seeds and add avocado before serving.

6

SERVES 4 TO 6
ACTIVE TIME: 30 MINUTES

PREP AHEAD

Shred romaine

Grate jicama

Dice bell pepper

Halve tomatoes

MAKE AHEAD

Refrigerate cooked chicken
up to 5 days

Refrigerate assembled
salads up to 3 days; place
dressing on bottom of
bowls or store separately

NOTES AND SHORTCUTS

Sub Green Goddess
Dressing (page 33) for ranch

Sub ground bison or beef
for chicken

Southwestern Chicken Bowls
with Avocado Ranch Dressing

2 pounds ground chicken

1 tablespoon tomato paste

2 tablespoons water

**1½ tablespoons Healthy in a
Hurry Taco Seasoning (page 37)**

**3 avocados; 1 halved, 2 halved
and sliced**

Juice of 1 lime

8 cups shredded romaine lettuce

1 small jicama, grated

**1 orange bell pepper,
seeded and diced**

1 pint cherry tomatoes, halved

**1 cup grain-free tortilla chips,
roughly crushed**

½ cup dairy-free ranch dressing

¼ cup cilantro leaves and stems

In a large skillet over medium-high heat, brown chicken. Stir in
tomato paste, water, and taco seasoning. Turn heat to low and
keep warm.

In a blender, combine ranch dressing, unsliced avocado, and lime
juice. Blend on high speed for 15 seconds, until smooth.

Arrange chicken, romaine, jicama, bell pepper, tomatoes, sliced
avocados, and chips in serving bowls. Drizzle with avocado-ranch
dressing and top with cilantro before serving.

Week 7

7

This week has a little bit of everything. First up, savor the ease of a no-boil pasta, a true one-pan wonder where the noodles cook as they bake.

Next, we'll put our Freezer Prepper hat on with a chicken stew. Whip up this dinner in a snap with your Instant Pot or slow cooker, then tuck away a freezer-ready second meal for a night when you're frantically trying to figure out dinner. This stew can go from rock-solid frozen to your table in fewer than 35 minutes.

Pizza night is always a winner in my house and a fallback dinner when I'm short on time with hard-to-please eaters. Choose between my speedy grain-free crust or opt for store-bought, then customize with your favorite toppings. This is a great way to use up leftover dairy-free cheeses, pesto, or veggies from the pasta bake, so you won't find any toppings added to your grocery list.

For a breakfast-for-dinner end to the week, I use a sheet pan to create the most delicious crispy smashed potatoes with spicy crumbled chorizo topped with soft-boiled eggs and a drizzle of spicy aioli.

MAKE AHEAD

UP TO 1 WEEK

- Roast vegetables for penne
- Make sauce for Thai stew
- Make aioli for smashed potatoes
- Make pizza crusts

UP TO 5 DAYS

- Boil and drain potatoes
- Soft-boil eggs

PREP AHEAD

- Whisk sauce for penne
- Stem, seed, and slice bell pepper into 1-inch strips
- Quarter and cut zucchini and summer squash into 1-inch cubes
- Quarter and cut eggplant into 1-inch cubes
- Peel and thinly slice 3 onions
- Shred kale
- Juice lemon (1½ teaspoons)
- Juice lime (4 teaspoons)
- Mince 4 garlic cloves
- Chop green onions

GROCERY LIST

PROTEIN

- Boneless, skinless chicken thighs or breasts 6 pounds
- Bulk chorizo sausage 1 pound

PRODUCE

- Baby creamer potatoes or white-fleshed sweet potatoes 2 pounds
- Chinese eggplant 1
- Fresh cilantro for garnishing
- Fresh lemon juice 1½ teaspoons
- Fresh lime juice 4 teaspoons
- Fresh parsley for sprinkling
- Garlic cloves 4
- Green onions 1 bunch
- Lacinato kale 1 bunch
- Mushrooms 1 (8-ounce) container
- Pizza toppings of your choice
- Red bell pepper 1
- Summer squash 1
- Yellow onions 3
- Zucchini 1

REFRIGERATOR

- Dairy-free cheese 4 ounces
- Dairy-free pesto 6 ounces
- Dairy-free ricotta or cream cheese 8 ounces
- Dill pickle juice ½ teaspoon
- Instant Pot Soft-Boiled Eggs (page 253) 6

FREEZER

- Cauliflower rice for serving
- Frozen stir-fry variety mixed vegetables 2 (16-ounce) packages

CUPBOARD & COUNTER

- Arrowroot powder ½ cup (60g)
- Avocado oil mayonnaise ⅓ cup
- Baking powder ¾ teaspoon
- Chickpea flour 1⅓ cups (145g)
- Coconut aminos ¼ cup
- Fish sauce ¼ cup
- Full-fat coconut milk 2 (13.5-ounce) cans
- Garlic powder ½ teaspoon
- Grain-free penne pasta 1 (12-ounce) box
- Ground ginger 1½ teaspoons
- Healthy in a Hurry Cajun Seasoning (page 37) 1 tablespoon
- Healthy in a Hurry Fries Seasoning Salt (page 36) ¾ teaspoon
- Healthy in a Hurry Mediterranean Seasoning (page 37) 2¼ teaspoons
- Hot sauce 1½ teaspoons
- Mild Thai red curry paste 1 cup
- Spicy or Dijon mustard 1½ teaspoons
- Tomato paste ⅔ cup
- Unsalted chicken bone broth 4 cups

7

PREP AHEAD

Whisk sauce

Cut and season vegetables

MAKE AHEAD

Roast vegetables and refrigerate up to 7 days

Refrigerate baked pasta up to 5 days

Refrigerate, unbaked, for 2 days. Freeze, unbaked, up to 6 months; defrost before baking

Freeze, baked, up to 4 months

NOTES AND SHORTCUTS

See grain-free pasta note on page 224.

Be sure the lid of your baking dish fits tightly; if steam escapes, the noodles may be undercooked.

I prefer chickpea pasta in this dish, but if using cassava pasta, keep in mind it continues to cook and absorb liquid well after it is pulled from oven; bake for 25 minutes to be safe

Substitute 4 cups cooked spaghetti squash for penne and decrease broth to 1 cup; bake, uncovered, for 10 minutes

Dairy-free cheese brands: Miyoko's mozzarella, Kite Hill ricotta, Violife feta

No-Boil Baked Pesto and Vegetable Penne

MEDITERRANEAN ROASTED VEGETABLES

1 red bell pepper, seeded and cut into 1-inch-wide strips

1 zucchini, quartered lengthwise and cut into 1-inch cubes

1 summer squash, quartered lengthwise and cut into 1-inch cubes

1 Chinese eggplant, cut into 1-inch cubes

1 (8-ounce) container mushrooms, sliced

½ yellow onion, sliced into 1-inch strips

2 tablespoons avocado oil

1 teaspoon sea salt

½ teaspoon cracked black pepper

2¼ teaspoons Healthy in a Hurry Mediterranean Seasoning (page 37)

4 cups unsalted chicken bone broth

8 ounces dairy-free ricotta or cream cheese

6 ounces dairy-free pesto

1 teaspoon sea salt

¼ teaspoon cracked black pepper

12-ounces grain-free penne pasta

4 ounces dairy-free cheese, chopped

1 cup packed shredded lacinato kale

Chopped parsley for sprinkling

Preheat oven to 400°F.

Make the vegetables: Place bell peppers, zucchini, summer squash, eggplant, mushrooms, and onion on a large baking sheet and toss with oil, salt, black pepper, and Mediterranean seasoning.

In a 3- to 4-quart Dutch oven with tightly fitted lid, whisk together broth, ricotta, pesto, salt, and black pepper. Stir in penne and half of cheese. Place a layer of parchment paper on top of dish and cover very tightly so no steam escapes.

Place vegetables and covered pasta dish in the oven. Bake until pasta is al dente, 26 to 28 minutes, and vegetables are tender. Uncover pasta dish, stir in kale, and sprinkle remaining cheese on top. Continue baking for 10 minutes, until pasta is tender but still a little chewy.

Sprinkle parsley over top before serving.

Thai-Style Chicken Stew

2 (13.5-ounce) cans full-fat coconut milk

⅔ cup tomato paste

1 cup mild Thai red curry paste

¼ cup fish sauce

¼ cup coconut aminos

4 teaspoons fresh lime juice

4 teaspoons sea salt

1½ teaspoons ground ginger

6 pounds boneless, skinless chicken thighs or breasts

2 yellow onions, thinly sliced

4 garlic cloves, minced

2 (16-ounce) packages frozen stir-fry variety mixed vegetables

Cauliflower rice for serving

Fresh cilantro for garnishing

SERVES 6 NOW, 6 LATER
ACTIVE TIME: 35 MINUTES

PREP AHEAD

Prepare sauce

Slice onion

Mince garlic cloves

MAKE AHEAD

Refrigerate sauce
up to 3 weeks

Refrigerate, uncooked, up to 3 days; cooked, up to 1 week

Freeze, cooked, up to 4 months; uncooked, up to 6 months

NOTES AND SHORTCUTS

Add vegetables at same time as chicken for ease; just keep in mind they will be a bit mushy

Make one batch to cook now and a second batch to freeze for later.

In a medium bowl, whisk together coconut milk, tomato paste, curry paste, fish sauce, coconut aminos, lime juice, salt, and ginger into a sauce.

Equally divide chicken pieces between your cooking pot (slow cooker or Instant Pot) and a 9-inch glass container or freezer bag. Pour half of sauce into each container and equally divide the onion and garlic between them. Seal freezer container and store in freezer for later.

TO COOK NOW

Instant Pot: Secure lid and set valve to seal. Cook chicken mixture on high pressure with a 10-minute timer. Let pressure release naturally. Stir in 1 package frozen vegetables, cover, and allow steam to cook vegetables for 10 minutes.

Slow Cooker: Cook chicken mixture on low for 6 hours or high for 3 hours. Stir in 1 package frozen vegetables and cook for 1 hour longer.

Serve hot over cauliflower rice garnished with cilantro.

TO COOK LATER

Instant Pot: Remove container from freezer and allow to thaw just enough to remove contents. Cook as directed above but use a 30-minute timer.

Slow Cooker: Remove container from freezer and allow to thaw completely. Cook as directed above.

7

MAKES 2 (9-INCH) CRUSTS
ACTIVE TIME: 35 MINUTES

MAKE AHEAD

Load and freeze prebaked crusts with any dinner leftovers or any chosen toppings. Wrap tightly and freeze up to 4 months; cook from frozen at 425°F for 10 to 12 minutes.

NOTES AND SHORTCUTS

Sub Banza plain pizza, Cappello's naked pizza crust, or grain-free tortillas for homemade crust

Chickpea flour or garbanzo bean flour adds protein and body to this crust. I use sprouted chickpea flour for easier digestion. Thrive Market, PureLiving, or To Your Health all sell it.

Sub ⅔ cup (80g) cassava flour for chickpea flour

Pizza Night

1⅓ cups (145g) chickpea flour

½ cup (60g) arrowroot powder

¾ cup (175ml) warm water

3 tablespoons extra-virgin olive oil

¾ teaspoon baking powder

½ teaspoon garlic powder

½ teaspoon sea salt

2 tablespoons avocado oil

Toppings (recipes follow) of your choice

Place a 10-inch cast-iron skillet in oven and preheat to 500°F.

In a small bowl, whisk together chickpea flour, arrowroot powder, water, olive oil, baking powder, garlic powder, and salt. Let batter rest for 5 minutes, then whisk again.

Carefully remove hot skillet from oven, add 1 tablespoon avocado oil, and swirl to coat. Pour 1 cup batter into skillet, tilting skillet from side to side so batter almost reaches edges. Bake for 4 minutes. Remove crust from pan and repeat with remaining 1 tablespoon avocado oil and remaining 1 cup batter.

Spread sauce evenly on crusts, then divide toppings between the crusts. Bake directly on the oven rack for 3 to 5 minutes, until toppings are hot and bubbling.

Serve hot.

TOPPINGS

Roasted Vegetables and Honey Ricotta
⅓ cup tomato pizza sauce + ⅓ cup Mediterranean Roasted Vegetables (page 118) + ½ cup ricotta + 1 teaspoon honey + 1 teaspoon thyme

BBQ Chicken
1 cup BBQ sauce + 1 cup shredded rotisserie chicken + ¼ cup thinly sliced red onion + ¼ cup cilantro + 1 cup shredded cheese of choice

Pesto Sausage
1 cup pesto + 1 cup sliced Italian sausage + ¼ cup chopped sun-dried tomatoes + 1 cup shredded cheese of choice

Smashed Potatoes and Chorizo with Jammy Eggs

1 pound bulk chorizo sausage, crumbled

2 pounds baby creamer potatoes or cubed white-fleshed sweet potatoes

¾ teaspoon coarse sea salt

¾ teaspoon Healthy in a Hurry Fries Seasoning Salt (page 36)

¼ teaspoon cracked black pepper

CAJUN AIOLI

⅓ cup avocado oil mayonnaise

1½ teaspoons spicy or Dijon mustard

1 tablespoon Healthy in a Hurry Cajun Seasoning (page 37)

1½ teaspoons hot sauce

1½ teaspoons fresh lemon juice

½ teaspoon dill pickle juice

2 green onions, trimmed and white and green parts chopped

6 Instant Pot Soft-Boiled Eggs (page 253), halved

PREP AHEAD

Boil and cool potatoes; refrigerate up to 3 days

Chop green onions

MAKE AHEAD

Prepare and refrigerate aioli up to 2 weeks

Refrigerate up to 5 days; reheat in a 300°F oven for 10 to 15 minutes

NOTES AND SHORTCUTS

Sub sweet potatoes for creamer potatoes

Sub chopped bacon for chorizo

Sub 1 pound ground pork plus ½ packet Siete chorizo seasoning for chorizo

Sub any ground breakfast sausage for chorizo

Sub Everything Bagel seasoning or your favorite meat and potatoes seasoning for fries seasoning salt

To amp up store-bought mayo for aioli: Whisk together ⅓ cup Primal Kitchen Chipotle Lime Mayo, plus dill pickle juice and water to thin

Preheat oven to 450°F. Line a half sheet pan with parchment paper.

Add chorizo to prepared pan and place in oven while potatoes cook.

Meanwhile, in a large pot over medium-high heat, combine potatoes and ½ teaspoon salt and add water to cover. Bring to a boil, then turn heat to low and let simmer for 15 minutes, until potatoes are fork-tender. Drain.

Remove sheet pan from oven, add potatoes, and toss with chorizo to coat in rendered fat. Using a heavy measuring cup or a drinking glass, firmly smash potatoes, then sprinkle with fry seasoning salt, remaining ¼ teaspoon salt, and black pepper. Spread in an even layer and roast for 26 to 28 minutes, tossing halfway through, until potatoes are crisp and golden brown and chorizo is crisp.

To make aioli: In a small bowl, gently stir together mayonnaise, mustard, Cajun seasoning, hot sauce, lemon juice, and pickle juice.

Drizzle potatoes and chorizo with aioli, sprinkle with green onions, and arrange eggs around pan.

Serve hot.

Week 8

8

We begin this week with a one-skillet Korean-inspired beef bowl that is, without fail, devoured in my house. Humble ground beef harmonizes with an enticing pineapple-laced BBQ sauce and is served with an array of toppings.

The lamb keftedes recipe is an ode to an appetizer at my favorite local Greek date-night spot; it's an irresistible blend of lamb and spices and can be made well in advance. Convenience comes into play here by calling for a jar of store-bought marinara and frozen meatballs, then elevating the flavors with a few simple spice blends for a meal that looks entirely homemade but isn't.

A recipe that helps you clean out your fridge is a great way to end the week, and my meal-prep bowls transform leftover ingredients into a hearty meal that can be served for dinner or saved for lunches the next day. With a bunch of fresh mint and a head of garlic employed resourcefully throughout the recipes, this week promises convenience and bold flavors.

MAKE AHEAD

UP TO 1 WEEK

- Make dressing for meal-prep bowls
- Make spicy marinara sauce
- Make meatballs (if using homemade)
- Make BBQ sauce for beef bowls
- Make salsa for halibut

UP TO 5 DAYS

- Brown ground beef for beef bowls
- Roast vegetables for meal-prep bowls
- Dress and massage kale for meal-prep bowls

UP TO 1 DAY

- Thaw meatballs (if frozen)

PREP AHEAD

- Mince 6 garlic cloves
- Slice 1 bunch green onions
- Wash and shred lettuce
- Slice 3 cucumbers
- Scrub and quarter potatoes
- Zest lemon
- Juice lemons
- Wash and chop mint, cilantro, and dill; refrigerate with wet paper towel gently draped over top
- Break broccoli or cauliflower into florets
- Peel and cube vegetables

GROCERY LIST

PROTEIN

- Ground beef **2 pounds**
- Halibut fillets, about 1 inch thick **2 (8-ounce)**
- Large shrimp, peeled and deveined **1 pound**

PRODUCE

- Avocado **optional topping**
- Chopped fresh herbs, such as parsley, cilantro, or mint **optional topping**
- Cucumber **3 Persian or 1 English**
- Fresh cilantro **1 bunch**
- Fresh dill **1 bunch**
- Fresh flat-leaf parsley **1 bunch**
- Lemons **2**
- Fresh mint leaves **1 bunch**
- Garlic cloves **6**
- Green leaf lettuce **1 head**
- Green onions **1 bunch**
- Lacinato kale **1 bunch**
- Mixed vegetables (whatever you have on hand) **3 pounds**
- Red potatoes **1 pound**
- Rosemary sprigs **2**

REFRIGERATOR

- Crumbled dairy-free feta cheese **½ cup**
- Lamb meatballs (see page 34) **2 pounds**

FREEZER

- Grain-free pizza crust **1**

CUPBOARD & COUNTER

- Canned pineapple chunks **1 can**
- Castelvetrano green olives **½ cup**
- Chili powder **¾ teaspoon**
- Coconut aminos **½ cup**
- Everything Bagel seasoning **optional topping**
- Ghee **2 tablespoons**
- Ginger **¼-inch piece**
- Ground cumin **¼ teaspoon**
- Healthy in a Hurry Burnt Broccoli Seasoning (page 36) **2½ teaspoons**
- Healthy in a Hurry Cajun Seasoning (page 37) **3 teaspoons**
- Hulled hemp hearts **optional topping**
- Kimchi **½ cup**
- Large pitted dates **6**
- Marinara sauce **1 (24-ounce) jar**
- Pure maple syrup **2 tablespoons**
- Red pepper flakes **¼ teaspoon**
- Sauerkraut **optional topping**
- Sesame seeds **1 teaspoon, plus more for optional topping**
- Sriracha aioli **for serving**
- Tahini **½ cup**
- Toasted sesame oil **2 tablespoons**

8

Korean-Inspired BBQ Beef Bowls

SERVES 4 TO 6
ACTIVE TIME: 18 MINUTES

PREP AHEAD

Slice green onions

Shred lettuce

Slice cucumber

MAKE AHEAD

Prepare and refrigerate sauce up to 1 week

Brown ground beef and refrigerate up to 1 week. Store sauce separately.

NOTES AND SHORTCUTS

Sub store-bought sauce, such as Kevin's Korean BBQ sauce or Primal Kitchen Thick & Sticky Honey Teriyaki

It's important to use canned pineapple instead of fresh here. The enzymes in fresh pineapple are much stronger and can cause the protein in the meat to break down too much, causing it to become mushy.

Sub ground chicken or turkey for beef

Sub store-bought spicy mayonnaise or mix together ½ cup mayonnaise, 2 tablespoons sriracha, juice of 1 lime, 1 teaspoon sea salt, and ¾ teaspoon cayenne pepper for sriracha aioli; refrigerate up to 1 month

BBQ SAUCE

⅓ cup canned pineapple chunks, juices drained

½ cup coconut aminos

6 large pitted dates

4 green onions, white parts, sliced

3 garlic cloves

¼-inch piece ginger, peeled

2 tablespoons toasted sesame oil

1 teaspoon fine sea salt

¼ teaspoon cracked black pepper

¼ teaspoon red pepper flakes

1 head green leaf lettuce, shredded

3 Persian or 1 English cucumber, thinly sliced

½ cup kimchi

Sriracha aioli for serving

2 pounds ground beef

4 green onions, sliced, white and green parts separated

1 teaspoon sesame seeds

To make sauce: In a blender or food processor, combine pineapple, coconut aminos, dates, white parts of green onions, garlic, ginger, sesame oil, salt, black pepper, and red pepper flakes and process until smooth. Set aside.

Place lettuce and cucumber slices on a large cutting board, along with kimchi and aioli in small serving bowls.

In a large skillet over high heat, cook ground beef with white parts of green onions for 5 to 7 minutes, breaking up with a wooden spoon, until fully browned. Drain the fat. Turn heat to low, drizzle in sauce, and let simmer for 3 to 5 minutes, until thickened. Sprinkle with sesame seeds and green parts of green onions.

Serve immediately from skillet (to keep meat hot) in bowls with lettuce, cucumbers, kimchi, and aioli for topping.

Roasted Halibut with Potatoes and Lemon-Olive Salsa

1 pound red potatoes, scrubbed and quartered

1 tablespoon, plus 3 teaspoons avocado oil

Sea salt and cracked black pepper

2 (8-ounce) halibut fillets, about 1 inch thick

¾ teaspoon chili powder

2 rosemary sprigs

LEMON-OLIVE SALSA

½ cup Castelvetrano green olives, pitted and coarsely chopped

2 tablespoons extra-virgin olive oil

Zest and juice of 1 Meyer lemon

1 garlic clove, minced

1 tablespoon chopped flat-leaf parsley leaves and tender stems

1 tablespoon chopped mint leaves

1 tablespoon chopped dill

1 pinch coarse sea salt

8

SERVES 4 TO 6
ACTIVE TIME: 35 MINUTES

PREP AHEAD

Scrub and quarter potatoes

MAKE AHEAD

Refrigerate salsa up to 1 week

NOTES AND SHORTCUTS

Sub cod for halibut

Sub 2 pounds bone-in skin-on chicken thighs for halibut

Sub cubed Hannah or other white-fleshed sweet potatoes for potatoes

Sub 2 regular lemons for Meyer lemon

Sub oregano or thyme for rosemary

Sub store-bought tapenade with a squeeze of fresh lemon juice for salsa

Preheat oven to 450°F.

Place potatoes on a half sheet pan and drizzle with 1 tablespoon avocado oil and a generous pinch of salt and black pepper. Push potatoes to outer edges of pan in an even layer and bake for 15 minutes.

Remove pan from oven. Place fillets in center of baking sheet, drizzle with 1 teaspoon avocado oil, and season with chili powder and a generous pinch of salt. Top each fillet with a rosemary sprig. Drizzle again with remaining 2 teaspoons avocado oil and return to oven. Bake for 10 to 12 minutes, until fish is just opaque and potatoes are golden.

To make salsa: While fish is baking, in a small bowl, stir together olives, olive oil, lemon zest and juice, garlic, parsley, mint, dill, and salt.

Spoon salsa over fillets and serve hot.

8

SERVES 4 TO 6

ACTIVE TIME: 25 MINUTES

PREP AHEAD

Thaw meatballs in refrigerator overnight

Chop mint and cilantro; refrigerate with wet paper towel gently draped over top

MAKE AHEAD

Refrigerate 1 week or freeze 6 months. Prep pizza crust and add herbs just before serving.

Refrigerate sauce up to 2 weeks

Make meatballs up to 4 months

NOTES AND SHORTCUTS

Sub any store-bought or homemade Cajun seasoning for Healthy in a Hurry brand

Omit feta or sub sheep's milk feta for dairy-free cheese

Dairy-free feta brands: Trader Joe's and Violife

Make my quick cast-iron pizza crust (see page 122) or purchase a grain-free brand, such as Banza plain crust pizza or Cappello's naked pizza

Lamb meatballs are difficult to come by in the grocery store, so feel free to sub any type of meatball here. Meatball brands: Amylu Foods, Aidells, Cooked Perfect, Sprouts, Trader Joe's

Lamb Keftedes with Spicy Marinara

Avocado oil for frying

2 pounds lamb meatballs (see page 34), thawed if frozen

1 (24-ounce) jar marinara sauce

⅓ cup, plus 1 tablespoon extra-virgin olive oil

3 teaspoons Healthy in a Hurry Cajun Seasoning (page 37)

1 grain-free pizza crust

1 pinch coarse sea salt

½ cup crumbled dairy-free feta cheese

¼ cup chopped mint leaves

¼ cup chopped cilantro leaves and tender stems

Line a large plate with paper towels.

In a large deep skillet over medium-high heat, warm ½ inch avocado oil until it shimmers. Add meatballs, in batches, in a single layer and fry for 3 to 4 minutes, turning occasionally, until browned and heated through. Using a slotted spoon, remove meatballs to prepared plate to drain.

Preheat oven to broil.

In a medium saucepan over low heat, combine marinara sauce, ⅓ cup olive oil, and Cajun seasoning and cook for 5 to 7 minutes, until sauce is gently simmering around edges.

Meanwhile, place pizza crust directly on the rack under broiler and toast for 1 to 2 minutes, until golden. Brush with remaining 1 tablespoon olive oil and sprinkle with salt. Slice into wedges.

Spread sauce in a shallow bowl, add meatballs, and top with feta, mint, and cilantro.

Serve with crust wedges alongside.

Fridge Clean-Out Veggie and Shrimp Meal-Prep Bowls

8

SERVES 4 TO 6
ACTIVE TIME: 45 MINUTES

3 pounds mixed vegetables

2 tablespoons avocado oil

2 tablespoons ghee, melted

1 tablespoon fresh lemon juice

2½ teaspoons Healthy in a Hurry Burnt Broccoli Seasoning (page 36)

1 teaspoon sea salt

½ teaspoon cracked black pepper

1 pound large shrimp, peeled and deveined

LEMON-TAHINI DRESSING

½ cup tahini

2 tablespoons fresh lemon juice

2 tablespoons pure maple syrup

2 garlic cloves, minced

½ teaspoon sea salt

¼ teaspoon ground cumin

1 bunch lacinato kale, stemmed and shredded

1 tablespoon extra-virgin olive oil

1 teaspoon fresh lemon juice

½ teaspoon sea salt

Sliced avocado, sauerkraut, hulled hemp hearts or sesame seeds, and Everything Bagel seasoning for topping (optional)

Chopped fresh herbs for sprinkling (optional)

PREP AHEAD

Peel and cube vegetables

Dress and massage kale

MAKE AHEAD

Refrigerate dressing up to 1 month

Refrigerate cooked shrimp up to 3 days

Refrigerate composed bowls, dressing and shrimp separately, up to 5 days. Serve cold or reheat a single container in a 400°F oven set for 10 minutes. Add cold or gently rewarmed shrimp and other toppings.

NOTES AND SHORTCUTS

Sub ¾ teaspoon sea salt and ⅛ teaspoon cracked black pepper for Burnt Broccoli Seasoning

Sub avocado oil for ghee

Use whatever lingering vegetables you have in your crisper or potato drawer; I love a combination of butternut, parsnips, mushrooms, and broccoli

Sub roasted salmon, meatballs, or leftover chicken for shrimp

Preheat oven to 425°F. Line a half sheet pan or two half sheet pans with parchment paper.

Place vegetables on prepared sheet pan(s) and drizzle with avocado oil, 1 tablespoon ghee, and lemon juice. Sprinkle with broccoli seasoning, ½ teaspoon salt, and ¼ teaspoon black pepper, and toss.

Roast for 25 minutes, tossing halfway through, until vegetables are lightly browned and crisp.

Toss shrimp in remaining 1 tablespoon ghee and season with remaining ½ teaspoon salt and remaining ¼ teaspoon black pepper. Push vegetables to side of pan(s) and add shrimp in a single layer. Roast for 2 to 3 minutes longer, until shrimp are pink throughout.

To make dressing: In a small bowl, whisk together tahini, lemon juice, maple syrup, garlic, salt, and cumin. Thin with water, if needed.

In a medium bowl, combine kale, olive oil, lemon juice, and salt. Using your hands, massage kale leaves until softened slightly and liquids are absorbed.

Remove vegetables from oven and divide among bowls. Fill each bowl with kale salad, shrimp, and desired toppings. Drizzle with 1 to 2 tablespoons dressing and fresh herbs.

Week 9

9

Your Batch Cooker persona will be in full effect this week, as you prepare a batch of creamy root vegetable mash to use in both the cottage pie and the meatballs marsala. You'll use two-thirds of it in the pie (one batch for dinner and another for your freezer stash!) and the remaining one-third as a side dish with the meatballs at the end of the week.

This week of Italian-inspired dishes pays homage to two culinary legends in my life, Grandma Marge and Great-Granny Sarella. Great-Granny Sarella's meat sauce simmers away all day, while you're running errands or at work. Some is served over grain-free noodles for dinner one night and the rest will be used as components to morph into two other meals.

My minestrone soup uses some of that long-simmered sauce to add both protein and flavor! And your week will end with a rich meatball dish that combines premade frozen meatballs with a silky marsala sauce served over those mashed root veggies you saved from earlier in the week. It may seem as if you have a lot to do up front this week, but get ready to experience the joys and efficiencies of batch cooking and freezer-ready solutions.

MAKE AHEAD

UP TO 1 WEEK
- Make meatballs (if using homemade)

UP TO 5 DAYS
- Make meat sauce or thaw from freezer; see also sauce shortcut page 146
- Make mashed roots

UP TO 3 DAYS
- Boil and drain spaghetti noodles
- Cook and drain elbow noodles for minestrone

UP TO 1 DAY
- Thaw meatballs in refrigerator

PREP AHEAD
- Chop 2 onions
- Mince 6 garlic cloves
- Peel and cube parsnips and turnips
- Chop bell pepper
- Chop kale
- Stem and halve mushrooms
- Mince shallots
- Chop parsley and basil

GROCERY LIST

PROTEIN

- Ground beef 3 pounds
- Prosciutto 4 ounces
- Thick-cut bone-in pork chops 3 pounds

PRODUCE

- Cremini mushrooms 8 ounces
- Curly kale 3 cups
- Fresh basil 1 bunch
- Flat-leaf parsley 1 bunch
- Garlic cloves 6
- Green bell pepper 1
- Parsnips 3 pounds
- Small shallots 2
- Turnips 1½ pounds
- Yellow onions 2

REFRIGERATOR

- Dairy-free Parmesan cheese for serving (optional)

FREEZER

- Cooked chicken meatballs (see page 34) 2 pounds
- Frozen mixed vegetables 5 cups
- Frozen shredded hash browns 1 (12-ounce) package

CUPBOARD & COUNTER

- Arrowroot powder 2 tablespoons
- Coconut aminos 1 tablespoon
- Dried oregano 3 tablespoons
- Ghee 1 cup plus 2 tablespoons
- Grain-free elbow noodles 1 (8-ounce) box
- Grain-free spaghetti noodles 2 (8-ounce) boxes
- Ground cinnamon ¾ teaspoon
- Honey 2 tablespoons
- Italian seasoning 1 teaspoon
- Strained tomatoes 3 (24-ounce) jars
- Sweet marsala wine ½ cup
- Sweet paprika ½ teaspoon
- Tomato paste 1 (7-ounce) jar
- Unsalted beef bone broth 8 cups
- Unsalted chicken bone broth 3 cups

9

MAKES 8 CUPS

ACTIVE TIME: 35 MINUTES

NOTES AND SHORTCUTS

Sub Instant Pot Mashed
Potatoes (page 273) for
mashed roots

Sub sweet potatoes or
russet potatoes for parsnips
or turnips

Sub grass-fed butter or
avocado oil for ghee

Prep Recipe: Mashed Roots

**3 pounds parsnips, peeled
and cubed**

**1½ pounds turnips, peeled
and cubed**

**1½ cups unsalted chicken
bone broth**

⅔ cup ghee

3 teaspoons fine sea salt

**1½ teaspoons freshly
ground black pepper**

Fill a large pot with cold water and add parsnips and turnips. Bring
to a boil over high heat, partially cover, then turn heat to medium
and cook for 15 minutes, until parsnips and turnips are fork-tender.
Drain vegetables and transfer to a food processor. Add broth,
ghee, salt, and black pepper and puree until smooth. Cool to room
temperature and store, tightly covered, in the refrigerator for
10 days; freeze for 6 months.

9

SERVES 4 NOW, 4 LATER
ACTIVE TIME: 20 MINUTES (PLUS
8 HOURS SLOW-COOKING TIME)

PREP AHEAD

Chop onion

Mince garlic cloves

Boil and drain noodles

MAKE AHEAD

Refrigerate sauce up
to 1 week; freeze up to
6 months

NOTES AND SHORTCUTS

Use thick-cut pork chops,
so bones don't fragment
during long cooking process.
If you use thin-cut, pull
them out halfway through
cooking process.

Look for jars or boxes
of passata or strained
tomatoes when shopping.
Pomi and Bionaturae are
my favorite brands.

Sub ¼ cup dried parsley
for fresh

Sub cooked spaghetti
squash noodles for dried
noodles (see page 221)

Scan code for a recipe using
cooked pork chops

Granny's Spaghetti with Meat Sauce

GRANNY'S MEAT SAUCE

2 tablespoons extra-virgin
olive oil

3 pounds thick-cut bone-in
pork chops

3 pounds ground beef

2 cups unsalted beef bone broth

2 yellow onions, chopped

6 garlic cloves, minced

3 (24-ounce) jars strained
tomatoes

1 (7-ounce) jar tomato paste

2 tablespoons honey

¼ cup chopped basil

3 tablespoons dried oregano

1 tablespoon sea salt

¾ teaspoon cracked black pepper

½ cup chopped flat-leaf parsley

¾ teaspoon ground cinnamon

2 (8-ounce) boxes grain-free
spaghetti noodles

Make one batch to cook now and a second batch to use in Cheats
Minestrone (page 146) and Italian Cottage Pie (page 149) or to freeze
for later.

TO COOK NOW

In a Dutch oven over medium-high heat, warm oil until it shimmers.
Add pork chops and brown well on all sides, 3 to 5 minutes. Using
tongs, transfer pork chops to a slow cooker insert.

Add ground beef to Dutch oven and brown for 5 to 7 minutes. Transfer
to slow cooker with about half of juices and discard remaining juices.

Add broth, onions, garlic, strained tomatoes, tomato paste, honey,
basil, oregano, salt, and black pepper to slow cooker. Stir, cover, and
cook on low for 8 hours or high for 4 hours.

Remove pork chops for another use. Stir in parsley and cinnamon.
Just before sauce is ready, cook 1 package spaghetti according to
package instructions and drain.

Pour half of sauce over noodles and serve hot. Pour remaining
sauce into a 9-inch glass container or freezer bag. Let cool, seal,
and refrigerate for use later this week or freeze for later.

TO COOK LATER

Remove container from freezer.

Instant Pot: Once thawed just enough to remove contents, add
to Instant Pot, secure lid, and set valve to seal. Cook on high pressure
with a 10-minute timer. Let pressure release naturally for 10 minutes,
then quick-release remaining pressure. Serve with cooked spaghetti.

9

SERVES 4 TO 6

ACTIVE TIME: 25 MINUTES

PREP AHEAD

Chop bell pepper

Chop kale

Cook and drain noodles

Thaw Granny's Meat Sauce (see page 144) or mix up shortcut sauce (see following)

MAKE AHEAD

Refrigerate up to 5 days

Freeze up to 6 months

NOTES AND SHORTCUTS

Cascadian Farm sells an organic blend of shredded frozen potatoes, carrots, and sweet potatoes that works wonderfully here, as will 8 ounces potatoes and 8 ounces carrots, peeled and grated with a food processor or box grater.

Al dente means "to the tooth" and is an Italian term used to describe pasta that is slightly undercooked and still has a bit of a bite to it. Use al dente cassava, chickpea, or spaghetti squash noodles.

Sub 2 cups store-bought marinara sauce and 1 pound browned ground beef for Granny's meat sauce

Sub frozen cauliflower rice for pasta

Cheats Minestrone

1 (8-ounce) box grain-free elbow noodles

6 cups unsalted beef bone broth

2 cups Granny's Meat Sauce (see page 144)

1 (12-ounce) package frozen shredded hash browns

1 green bell pepper, seeded and chopped

3 cups chopped curly kale

1 teaspoon sea salt

½ teaspoon cracked black pepper

½ teaspoon sweet paprika

Dairy-free Parmesan cheese and parsley for serving (optional)

In a medium stockpot, cook noodles according to package instructions until al dente. Drain and set aside.

Return the pot to the stove over medium-high heat, combine broth and sauce and bring to a boil. Stir in hash browns, bell pepper, kale, salt, black pepper, and paprika. Turn heat to medium and let simmer for 8 to 10 minutes, until bell pepper is soft. Stir in noodles and turn off heat.

Sprinkle with Parmesan and parsley, if desired, before serving.

Italian Cottage Pie

5 cups frozen mixed vegetables, defrosted

6 cups Granny's Meat Sauce (see page 144)

½ cup unsalted chicken bone broth

1 tablespoon coconut aminos

1 teaspoon Italian seasoning

Sea salt and cracked black pepper

6 cups Mashed Roots (page 142)

¼ cup melted ghee

¼ cup chopped parsley or basil

TO COOK NOW

Preheat oven to 400°F. Lightly grease two 9 by 13-inch baking dishes.

In a large bowl, mix together frozen vegetables, sauce, broth, coconut aminos, Italian seasoning, 1½ teaspoons salt, and ½ teaspoon black pepper. Season with additional salt and pepper, if needed.

Equally divide sauce and veggie mixture between prepared baking dishes. Then divide mashed roots between the two dishes and carefully smooth to cover sauce. Drag tines of a fork across top to make decorative ridges. Brush ghee over top.

Tightly wrap one casserole and store in the freezer for later.

Cover the second casserole and bake for 20 to 25 minutes, until filling is bubbling. Remove cover, turn oven to broil, slightly prop open oven door, and broil for 3 to 5 minutes, until potatoes are golden brown and have a slight crust.

Sprinkle parsley over top and serve hot.

TO COOK LATER

Preheat oven to 375°F. Remove casserole from freezer and bake, covered, for 1 to 1½ hours, until filling is bubbling. Finish as directed above.

SERVES 6 NOW, 6 LATER

ACTIVE TIME: 35 MINUTES

PREP AHEAD

Defrost sauce in fridge overnight, if frozen

MAKE AHEAD

Refrigerate up to 5 days; freeze up to 4 months

NOTES AND SHORTCUTS

Sub any store-bought marinara sauce, such as Rao's, and 1 pound browned beef, turkey, or lamb for Granny's Meat Sauce

I like to use a mix of carrots, onions, green beans, and green peas but feel free to use whatever frozen vegetables your family prefers

For a shortcut, use good-quality, premade mashed potatoes or mashed cauliflower from Alexia brand. Stir in an egg yolk before piping on top of meat sauce for added richness and moisture, since store-bought can be a bit dry.

To make just enough mashed roots for this recipe, halve the prep recipe on page 142.

Sub avocado oil for ghee

9

SERVES 4 TO 6
ACTIVE TIME: 20 MINUTES

PREP AHEAD

Thaw meatballs, if frozen

Stem and halve mushrooms

Mince shallots

Chop parsley

MAKE AHEAD

Refrigerate meatballs, uncooked, up to 3 days; cooked, up to 1 week

Freeze meatballs, cooked, up to 4 months; uncooked, up to 6 months

Refrigerate meatballs, sauce, and mashed roots separately, up to 1 week

NOTES AND SHORTCUTS

Sub butter or avocado oil for ghee

Sub ¼ cup white grape juice, plus 1 teaspoon vanilla extract and 2 tablespoons sherry vinegar for Marsala

Sub Madeira wine for Marsala

Sub cubed chicken thighs for meatballs

Meatball brands: Amylu Foods, Aidells, Cooked Perfect, Sprouts, Trader Joe's

Sub porcini mushrooms for cremini

Meatballs Marsala with Mashed Roots

¼ cup extra-virgin olive oil

2 pounds cooked chicken meatballs (see page 34), thawed if frozen

4 ounces prosciutto, thinly sliced

8 ounces cremini mushrooms, stemmed and halved

2 small shallots, minced

Sea salt and cracked black pepper

1 cup unsalted chicken bone broth

2 tablespoons arrowroot powder

½ cup sweet Marsala wine

2 tablespoons ghee

¼ cup chopped flat-leaf parsley

3 cups Mashed Roots (page 142)

In a large skillet over medium-high heat, warm oil until it shimmers. Add meatballs in an even layer and brown on all sides, about 6 minutes. Work in batches if needed. Remove meatballs from skillet and keep warm.

Turn heat to medium, add prosciutto to drippings in pan, and sauté for 1 minute. Add mushrooms and shallots and sauté until well browned and moisture has mostly evaporated, 5 to 7 minutes. Season with salt and pepper.

In a small bowl, whisk together broth and arrowroot powder to make a slurry.

Pour Marsala into pan and let boil for a few seconds to burn off alcohol. Add slurry and reduce heat to medium-low. Let simmer for 2 minutes to thicken sauce slightly. Stir in ghee and return meatballs to pan. Simmer for 2 to 3 minutes, until meatballs are heated through.

Season with salt and pepper and garnish with parsley. Serve mashed roots with meatballs and sauce spooned over top.

Week 10

10

The week kicks off with a versatile shredded beef dish that you quickly prepare in an Instant Pot and then use in the enchiladas as well as the breakfast tacos. These sister dishes showcase the rich depth of tender shredded beef, while offering variety without extensive cooking. You may have leftover beef at the end of the week, so throw it into the freezer and use it in Enchilada-Stuffed Sweet Potatoes (page 96).

If you are craving a light seafood dish with minimal prep, the smoked salmon delivers a healthful dose of omega-3s without the fear of overcooking the fish.

You get one meatless day this week with my dairy-free broccoli soup. It's so hearty and is especially delicious served with a big green salad and a toasted slice of your favorite grain-free bread.

MAKE AHEAD

UP TO 1 WEEK
- Make yogurt sauce for smoked salmon
- Make cheesy broccoli soup

UP TO 5 DAYS
- Cook chuck roast for shredded beef
- Make enchilada sauce

UP TO 3 DAYS
- Marinate asparagus for smoked salmon
- Soft-boil eggs for smoke salmon
- Fill and roll enchiladas in casserole

PREP AHEAD
- Chop 2 yellow onions, thinly slice 1
- Mince 1 red onion
- Chop chives and capers
- Trim asparagus
- Chop 8 garlic cloves
- Peel and cube sweet potatoes
- Peel and chop broccoli stems, cut tops into florets
- Chop 4 carrots
- Chop 4 celery stalks
- Dice zucchini
- Beat eggs
- Slice radishes and avocados

GROCERY LIST

PROTEIN

- Boneless chuck roast 4 to 5 pounds
- Smoked salmon 5 ounces

PRODUCE

- Asparagus 1 bunch
- Avocados 2
- Broccoli 1½ pounds
- Celery stalks 4
- Dill sprigs 2
- Fresh chives 1 small bunch
- Fresh cilantro 1 bunch
- Garlic cloves 8
- Green salad for serving
- Jalapeño 1
- Large lemon 1
- Lime 1
- Medium carrots 4
- Radishes 1 small bunch
- Red onion 1
- Shredded romaine lettuce (optional)
- Sliced avocado (optional)
- Sliced radishes (optional)
- White-fleshed sweet potatoes 1 pound
- Yellow onions 3
- Zucchini 1

REFRIGERATOR

- Chipotle aioli ¼ cup
- Dairy-free cream cheese 8 ounces
- Dairy-free sour cream for serving (optional)
- Eggs 1 dozen
- Grain-free tortillas 20
- Mild roasted tomatillo salsa 1 (16-ounce) container
- Plain unsweetened dairy-free yogurt 4 ounces
- Salsa of your choice ⅓ cup

CUPBOARD & COUNTER

- Apple cider vinegar 1 teaspoon
- Bay leaves 2
- Capers 2 teaspoons
- Coconut aminos 3 tablespoons
- Coconut cream ½ cup
- Everything Bagel seasoning ½ teaspoon
- Garlic powder 2 teaspoons
- Ghee 1 tablespoon
- Healthy in a Hurry Taco Seasoning (page 37) 1 tablespoon
- Honey 1 teaspoon
- Nutritional yeast 2 tablespoons
- Unsalted beef bone broth ¾ to 1 cup
- Unsalted vegetable broth 2 (32-ounce) boxes

10

SERVES 6 NOW, 6 LATER
ACTIVE TIME: 10 MINUTES
(PLUS 75 MINUTES PRESSURE-
COOKING TIME)

PREP AHEAD

Cut roast

Slice onion

MAKE AHEAD

Refrigerate up to 1 week

Freeze up to 4 months

NOTES AND SHORTCUTS

Sub flank steak for chuck
roast

Store meat in its juices so
it doesn't dry out when
reheating; drain the juices
before using in other
recipes

Use leftover beef in
Enchilada-Stuffed Sweet
Potatoes (page 96)

Prep Recipe: Shredded Beef

4 to 5 pounds boneless chuck roast, cut into 4 pieces

1 large yellow onion, thinly sliced

¾ cup to 1 cup unsalted beef bone broth

3 tablespoons coconut aminos

1 teaspoon apple cider vinegar

2½ teaspoons sea salt

2 teaspoons garlic powder

¾ teaspoon cracked black pepper

2 bay leaves

Make one batch to cook now and a second batch to use in Beef and Zucchini Enchiladas Verdes (page 163) and Steak and Eggs Breakfast Tacos (page 164) or to freeze for later.

In an Instant Pot set to sauté mode high or a Dutch oven set over high heat, add beef and sear on both sides for 2 to 3 minutes, until browned.

TO COOK NOW

Instant Pot: Add onion, ¾ cup broth, coconut aminos, vinegar, salt, garlic powder, black pepper, and bay leaves. Secure lid and set valve to seal. Cook on high pressure with a 60-minute timer. Let pressure release naturally for 15 minutes, then quick-release remaining pressure.

Slow Cooker: Transfer beef to a slow cooker and add onion, 1 cup broth, coconut aminos, vinegar, salt, garlic powder, black pepper, and bay leaves. Cook on low for 8 hours or on high for 4 hours.

Using an electric handheld mixer or two forks, shred beef in pot; retain juices.

Transfer half the beef and juices to a 9-inch glass container or freezer bag. Seal and store in the refrigerator to use later this week or in the freezer for later.

TO COOK LATER

Remove container from freezer.

Instant Pot: Once thawed just enough to remove contents, place in Instant Pot, secure lid, and set valve to seal. Cook as directed above but use a 20-minute timer.

Stovetop: Once thawed completely, place contents in a Dutch oven and warm over medium heat for 15 minutes.

Smoked Salmon with Roasted Asparagus and Lemon-Caper Yogurt

1 tablespoon avocado oil

Zest of 1 lemon, plus
2 tablespoons fresh lemon juice

1 teaspoon honey

½ teaspoon Everything Bagel seasoning

1 bunch asparagus, trimmed

4 ounces plain unsweetened dairy-free yogurt

2 tablespoons chopped chives

1 tablespoon finely minced red onion

2 teaspoons capers, drained and chopped

Sea salt and cracked black pepper

5 ounces smoked salmon

2 dill sprigs

4 soft-boiled eggs, halved

Preheat oven to 425°F.

In a small bowl, whisk together oil, lemon zest, 1 tablespoon lemon juice, honey, and bagel seasoning. Add asparagus and toss, then spread evenly on a baking sheet. Roast for 10 to 12 minutes, until crisp-tender.

Meanwhile, in another small bowl, mix together yogurt, remaining 1 tablespoon lemon juice, chives, red onion, capers, and a pinch each of salt and black pepper.

Arrange asparagus on a platter and flake salmon over top. Dollop with some yogurt mixture and garnish with dill and eggs.

Serve with remaining yogurt alongside.

10

SERVES 4
ACTIVE TIME: 20 MINUTES

PREP AHEAD

Make dressing

Trim asparagus

Mince onion

Chop chives and capers

MAKE AHEAD

Refrigerate yogurt mixture up to 10 days

Refrigerate composed dish up to 3 days

NOTES AND SHORTCUTS

I'm obsessed with this yogurt; I make a double batch and dollop it on everything from salads to fried eggs to a bowl of curry or soup

Sub roasted and cooled salmon, canned salmon, or smoked trout for smoked salmon

10

SERVES 6 TO 8
ACTIVE TIME: 18 MINUTES

PREP AHEAD

Chop onions and garlic

Chop celery

Cube sweet potatoes

Chop carrots

MAKE AHEAD

Refrigerate up to 10 days

Freeze up to 6 months

NOTES AND SHORTCUTS

I choose white-fleshed sweet potatoes (Hannah, Japanese, or boniato) because they are starchier and less sweet than a traditional orange-fleshed yam, but any variety will work here

I prefer Miyoko's cream cheese in this recipe

Sub Green Valley lactose-free cream cheese or Kite Hill ricotta

Sub 8 ounces raw cashews (soaked in boiling water and drained), 1 teaspoon apple cider vinegar, and 1 teaspoon lemon juice for cream cheese; blend with vegetables and broth

Cheesy Broccoli Soup

6 tablespoons avocado oil

2 small yellow onions, chopped

8 garlic cloves, chopped

1 pound white-fleshed sweet potatoes, peeled and cubed

4 celery stalks, chopped

4 medium carrots, chopped

2 (32-ounce) boxes unsalted vegetable broth

8 ounces dairy-free cream cheese

2 tablespoons nutritional yeast

Sea salt and cracked black pepper

1½ pounds broccoli, thick stems peeled and chopped, tops cut into small florets

Green salad for serving

In a large stockpot over medium heat, warm oil until it shimmers. Add onions and garlic and sauté for 3 to 4 minutes, stirring frequently, until fragrant and softened. Add sweet potatoes, celery, and carrots and continue to cook for 5 minutes longer. Pour in 1 box broth, turn heat to medium-high, and bring to a boil. Turn heat to low and let simmer for 6 to 8 minutes, until vegetables are fork-tender.

Carefully transfer vegetables and liquid to a blender. Add cream cheese, nutritional yeast, 2 teaspoons salt, and ½ teaspoon black pepper and blend on high speed until very smooth and creamy. Add broccoli and pulse three or four times, until broccoli is blended into bite-size pieces.

Return soup to stockpot and add remaining box broth. Turn heat to medium and let simmer for 3 to 5 minutes, until broccoli is bright green and tender. Season with salt and pepper.

Serve soup hot, with a green salad.

160   MAKE IT EASY

Beef and Zucchini
Enchiladas Verdes

SERVES 4 TO 6
ACTIVE TIME: 45 MINUTES

ENCHILADA SAUCE

1 (16-ounce) container mild roasted tomatillo salsa

½ cup coconut cream

1 avocado, pitted

¾ teaspoon sea salt

Juice of 1 small lime

1 small jalapeño, seeded

2 cups Shredded Beef (page 156), drained of juices

1 zucchini, diced

1 tablespoon Healthy in a Hurry Taco Seasoning (page 37)

12 grain-free tortillas, warmed slightly

Shredded romaine lettuce, sliced radishes, sliced avocado, chopped cilantro, minced red onion, dairy-free sour cream for serving (optional)

To make sauce: Reserve ⅓ cup salsa. In a blender, combine remaining salsa, coconut cream, avocado, salt, lime juice, and jalapeño. Puree on high speed until smooth. Set aside.

Preheat oven to 375°F.

In a large bowl, mix together beef, zucchini, reserved salsa, and taco seasoning.

Spread ½ cup sauce on bottom of a 9 by 13-inch baking dish. On a cutting board, stack warmed tortillas. Fill a tortilla with about ¼ cup beef filling, then carefully roll up and place seam-side down in baking dish. Repeat with remaining tortillas and filling. Pour sauce over filled enchiladas and place dish in oven.

Bake for 20 to 25 minutes, until edges are bubbling.

Serve topped with romaine, radishes, avocado, cilantro, onion, and sour cream, if desired.

PREP AHEAD

Dice zucchini

Prepare desired toppings

MAKE AHEAD

Refrigerate enchilada sauce up to 5 days; freeze up to 6 months

Refrigerate prepared enchiladas, sauce separately, up to 3 days; bake as instructed

Freeze prepared enchiladas, sauce separately, up to 4 months; defrost in fridge overnight and pour sauce over top before baking as instructed

NOTES AND SHORTCUTS

Sub rotisserie chicken or shredded pork (see page 104) for shredded beef

Sub browned and drained ground beef for shredded beef

Add 1 cup shredded jack cheese or 1 cup Cheesy Nacho Sauce (page 218) to beef mixture, if desired

Enchilada sauce brands: Siete and Sprouts

Use any grain-free taco seasoning; check for rice starch or other anti-caking agents

10

SERVES 4

ACTIVE TIME: 20 MINUTES

PREP AHEAD

Beat eggs

Slice avocado and radishes

MAKE AHEAD

Store components in fridge up to 5 days; fill tortillas with eggs and steak on a tray in an oven set to 350°F for 5 to 7 minutes, then add toppings

Cool fillings, then fill tortillas, wrap tightly, and freeze tacos up to 4 months. Reheat, from frozen, on a tray in an oven set to 350°F for 12 to 15 minutes. Add fresh toppings after reheating.

NOTES AND SHORTCUTS

Sub chopped bacon for shredded beef

Sub shredded pork (see page 104) for shredded beef

Sub avocado oil for ghee

Steak and Eggs Breakfast Tacos

8 grain-free tortillas

½ cup Shredded Beef (page 156), drained of juices

8 eggs

¼ teaspoon sea salt

1 tablespoon ghee

1 small bunch radishes, thinly sliced

¼ cup cilantro leaves and tender stems

⅓ cup salsa

1 avocado, sliced

¼ cup chipotle aioli

In a large skillet over medium-high heat, warm tortillas for 10 to 15 seconds on both sides. Transfer to a plate and cover with a kitchen towel to keep warm.

Turn heat to medium and add beef to skillet, stirring frequently until heated through. Transfer to a plate.

While beef is heating, use a fork to beat eggs together with salt in a small bowl.

Melt the ghee in the same skillet over medium heat, then pour in eggs and cook for 3 to 5 minutes, moving them around occasionally with a wooden spoon until mostly cooked through but still slightly loose. Push eggs to side and add beef back to pan. Turn heat to low to keep warm.

Divide eggs and beef among warmed tortillas. Top with radishes, cilantro, salsa, avocado slices, and aioli before serving.

Week 11

11

Get ready for a week of simplicity that doesn't skimp on flavor.
Up first is a rich and aromatic shrimp dish with sweet potatoes.
It offers mild curry flavors that come together with a handful of
pantry ingredients; you also have the option to make it vegetarian
or swap in chicken.

My creamy yet dairy-free mushroom soup pairs perfectly with
a crisp green salad and a slice of your favorite grain-free bread.
It's a wallet-friendly, meatless option that's both satisfying and
comforting.

The salmon cakes are a favorite flavor-packed protein that you
can enjoy over a salad all week long (if you happen to have any
left over). They are crafted from canned salmon for convenience,
and in the spirit of efficiency, I suggest you use a food processor
to chop all the vegetables, making meal preparation a breeze.

Cap off your week with sheet-pan fajitas, designed to serve double
duty: one batch for immediate enjoyment and another for your
freezer stash.

This week's meals prove that simplicity in the kitchen can coexist
with flavor and creativity.

MAKE AHEAD

UP TO 1 WEEK

- Make mushroom soup
- Chop vegetables for
  salmon cakes

UP TO 3 DAYS

- Make fajita freezer kits;
  freeze one

PREP AHEAD

- Mince ginger
- Mince 7 garlic cloves
- Shred sweet potatoes
  and refrigerate in a bowl
  of water
- Grind plantain chips
- Trim asparagus
- Juice 3 limes
- Slice 6 bell peppers
- Slice 2 yellow onions
- Chop 2 yellow onions
- Cut chicken strips

GROCERY LIST

PROTEIN

- Boneless, skinless chicken breasts 4 pounds
- Large shrimp, peeled and deveined 1½ pounds

PRODUCE

- Baby greens 5 cups
- Baby spinach 5 ounces
- Celery stalks 2
- Fresh cilantro for serving
- Fresh cilantro or basil for serving
- Fresh parsley 1 bunch
- Garlic cloves 7
- Ginger 1 small piece
- Green salad for serving
- Lemon wedges for serving
- Limes 4
- Medium sweet potatoes 2
- Medium yellow onions 4
- Mixed mushrooms 1 pound
- Multicolored bell peppers 6
- Small white onion 1
- Thick asparagus 1½ pounds

REFRIGERATOR

- Creamy dressing or aioli ¼ cup (optional)
- Dairy-free ricotta cheese 2 (8-ounce) containers
- Grain-free tortillas 12
- Guacamole for serving
- Salsa of your choice for serving

FREEZER

- Cauliflower rice for serving

CUPBOARD & COUNTER

- Artichoke hearts 1 cup
- Avocado oil mayonnaise ⅓ cup
- Capers 2 tablespoons
- Coconut oil 1 tablespoon
- Coconut sugar 2 tablespoons
- Dried thyme 1 teaspoon
- Dry sherry ¼ cup
- Fish sauce 2 teaspoons
- Full-fat coconut milk 1 (13.5-ounce) can
- Ghee 2 tablespoons
- Healthy in a Hurry Taco Seasoning (page 37) ½ cup
- Healthy in a Hurry Tagine Seasoning (page 37) 2 teaspoons
- Plantain chips 2 cups
- Red curry paste 1 tablespoon
- Roasted red peppers 1 cup
- Salmon 3 (6-ounce) cans
- Seafood seasoning 2 teaspoons
- Unsalted chicken bone broth 4 cups

11

PREP AHEAD

Shred sweet potatoes and refrigerate in a bowl of water up to 3 days

Mince ginger and garlic

MAKE AHEAD

Refrigerate up to 3 days

Freeze up to 3 months

NOTES AND SHORTCUTS

Sub honey for coconut sugar

Sub curry powder for tagine seasoning

Sub kabocha squash for sweet potatoes

Coconut-Curry Shrimp and Sweet Potatoes

2 medium sweet potatoes, peeled

1½ pounds large shrimp, peeled and deveined

2 tablespoons coconut sugar

2 teaspoons Healthy in a Hurry Tagine Seasoning (page 37)

1 tablespoon coconut oil

1 small piece ginger, minced

1 garlic clove, minced

1 (13.5-ounce) can full-fat coconut milk

1 tablespoon red curry paste

2 teaspoons fish sauce

Juice of 1 lime

5 ounces baby spinach, coarsely torn

Cauliflower rice for serving

Fresh cilantro or basil for serving

Using a box grater or food processor, shred sweet potatoes.

In a medium bowl, toss shrimp with 1 tablespoon coconut sugar and the tagine seasoning.

In a large skillet over medium-high heat, melt coconut oil. Add shrimp to skillet and cook for 2 to 3 minutes, stirring occasionally, until cooked through and no longer pink. Using a slotted spoon, remove from skillet and set aside.

Add ginger and garlic to skillet and sauté for 1 to 2 minutes, until fragrant. Pour in coconut milk and whisk to incorporate any browned bits. Whisk in red curry paste, remaining 1 tablespoon coconut sugar, fish sauce, and lime juice. Turn heat to low and let simmer for 8 to 10 minutes, until thick and reduced slightly. Remove from heat and stir in shrimp and spinach.

Serve over cauliflower rice and sprinkle cilantro or basil over top.

Cream of Mushroom Soup

¼ cup avocado oil

1 pound mixed mushrooms

2 medium yellow onions, coarsely chopped

6 garlic cloves

¼ cup dry sherry

4 cups unsalted chicken bone broth

2 (8-ounce) containers dairy-free ricotta cheese

1 teaspoon dried thyme

1½ teaspoons sea salt

½ teaspoon cracked black pepper

Green salad for serving

SERVES 6 TO 8
ACTIVE TIME: 18 MINUTES

MAKE AHEAD

Refrigerate up to 10 days

Freeze up to 6 months

TIPS AND SHORTCUTS

Freeze soup in ⅓-cup silicone muffin molds to use for cream of mushroom soup in your favorite casserole (see page 236)

Use a mix of at least two of following mushrooms: white button, shiitake, baby bella, and cremini

Sub frozen mushrooms for fresh; defrost and drain before using

Sub 2 tablespoons apple cider vinegar plus 2 tablespoons water for sherry

Sub dry vermouth for sherry

Sub vegetable broth for chicken broth

Kite Hill ricotta is my favorite brand for clean, dairy-free ricotta. If dairy is tolerated, sheep's milk ricotta by Bellwether Farms or buf brand ricotta made from buffalo milk are both lactose-free options

Sub Miyoko's dairy-free cream cheese for ricotta; omit sherry

In a stockpot over medium heat, warm oil until it shimmers. Add mushrooms, onions, and garlic and sauté for 8 to 10 minutes, or until mushrooms and onions have softened. Pour in sherry, turn heat to low, and let simmer for 2 to 3 minutes, until liquid has mostly evaporated.

In a blender, combine broth and ricotta and blend on high speed until smooth, about 30 seconds. Add mushroom mix, thyme, salt, and black pepper and pulse a few times, until mushrooms are bite-size but soup still has texture. Pour mixture back into pot, turn heat to medium, and let simmer until thickened, stirring frequently.

Serve hot, with a green salad on the side.

11

PREP AHEAD

Grind plantain chips

Quarter onion

Halve celery

Trim asparagus

MAKE AHEAD

Refrigerate, uncooked, up to 2 days; cooked, up to 5 days

Freeze up to 4 months

TIPS AND SHORTCUTS

Sub extra-virgin olive oil or butter for ghee

Sub ½ cup almond flour, crushed pork rind crumbs, or grain-free bread crumbs for plantain chips

To make a quick aioli—mix together ½ cup mayonnaise, 1 tablespoon Dijon mustard, the juice of 1 lemon, and a pinch of salt and black pepper

Green Goddess Dressing (page 33) also pairs well with this

Salmon Cakes and Roasted Artichokes and Asparagus

2 cups plantain chips

1 small white onion, quartered

2 celery stalks, halved

1 cup roasted red peppers

¼ cup packed parsley leaves

2 tablespoons melted ghee

⅓ cup avocado oil mayonnaise

2 tablespoons capers, drained

2 teaspoons seafood seasoning

¾ teaspoon sea salt

½ teaspoon cracked black pepper

3 (6-ounce) cans salmon

1½ pounds thick asparagus, trimmed

1 cup artichoke hearts, drained

1 tablespoon avocado oil

5 cups baby greens

Lemon wedges for serving

¼ cup aioli or creamy dressing (optional)

Preheat oven to 425°F and move rack to the top position. Line a half sheet pan with parchment paper.

In a food processor, process plantain chips until finely ground. Remove and set aside. Place onion, celery, roasted peppers, and parsley in food processor and pulse four or five times, until chopped. Add 1 tablespoon ghee, mayonnaise, capers, seafood seasoning, ½ teaspoon salt, and ¼ teaspoon black pepper and pulse again until just combined. Add salmon and plantain chip crumbs and pulse once or twice to incorporate.

Shape mixture into ten 2½- to 3-ounce cakes, about ½ inch thick. Arrange cakes in center of prepared sheet pan. Brush tops with remaining 1 tablespoon ghee. Place sheet pan on top rack of oven and bake for 10 minutes.

While cakes are baking, in a medium bowl, toss asparagus with artichoke hearts, oil, remaining ¼ teaspoon salt, and remaining ¼ teaspoon pepper.

After 10 minutes, flip cakes and scatter asparagus and artichoke hearts all around pan. Continue baking for 5 to 7 minutes longer, until cakes are browned and asparagus is crisp-tender.

Serve over greens with asparagus, artichokes, and lemon wedges alongside. Dollop with aioli, if desired.

Sheet-Pan Chicken Fajitas

4 pounds boneless, skinless chicken breasts, cut into ¼-inch strips

6 multicolored bell peppers, thinly sliced

2 medium yellow onions, halved and thinly sliced into half-moons

¼ cup avocado oil

¼ cup fresh lime juice

½ cup Healthy in a Hurry Taco Seasoning (page 37)

1 teaspoon sea salt

12 grain-free tortillas, warmed

Guacamole, salsa, cilantro, and lime wedges for serving

SERVES 4 NOW, 4 LATER
ACTIVE TIME: 25 MINUTES

PREP AHEAD

Cut chicken strips

Slice bell peppers

Slice onion

Juice limes

MAKE AHEAD

Refrigerate, uncooked, up to 3 days; cooked, up to 7 days

Freeze up to 4 months

NOTES AND SHORTCUTS

If cooking for a smaller crowd, divide freezer kit into two or three bags

Make one batch to cook now and a second batch to freeze for later.

In a large bowl, combine chicken, bell peppers, onion, oil, lime juice, taco seasoning, and salt and mix until chicken is well coated. Transfer half this mixture to a 9-inch glass container or freezer bag. Seal and store in the freezer for later. Cover the bowl and marinate the remaining mixture in the refrigerator for 1 hour.

TO COOK NOW

Set an oven rack 4 inches from heating element of oven. Place a half sheet pan on rack and preheat oven on broil setting. Carefully remove hot sheet pan from oven. Spread contents of bowl in an even layer, discarding marinade. Broil for 5 minutes, then toss and broil 3 to 5 minutes longer, until chicken is cooked through.

Serve in warm tortillas, topped with guacamole, salsa, cilantro, and lime wedges.

TO COOK LATER

Remove container from freezer and allow to thaw completely. Cook as directed above.

Week 12

12

This week I'm giving you two of the fallback meals I rely on the most: a quick stir-fry and a trusted meatball pasta. The lineup promises both convenience and satisfaction, catering to picky kids and busy schedules.

The lemon chicken is also a freezer kit, ensuring dinner tonight and an extra meal tucked away for future enjoyment. The zesty Greek flavors come together in an Instant Pot, and fresh yogurt and herbs liven it up at mealtime.

My second chicken dish is a grown-up version of a meal I loved as a kid: chicken nuggets, with the most incredible teriyaki-tomato dipping sauce and paired with a creamy macaroni salad that's a nod to our family's time living in Kona, Hawaii.

Midweek, we turn to a favorite stir-fry—a lifesaver on hectic sports nights. With just a few pounds of ground chicken, fresh veggies, and a simple sauce, it's a crowd-pleaser that never disappoints.

Finally, a dish that often comes to the rescue when my dinner plans go awry: the magical meatball pasta. It's a frequent visitor to our dinner table and to so many of yours, offering a comforting and flavorful solution for those "I forgot to plan dinner" moments.

With a mix of freezer kits, comforting classics, and dependable fallbacks, these meals prove that exceptional flavor and convenience can go hand in hand.

MAKE AHEAD

UP TO 1 WEEK

- Make stir-fry sauce
- Make mac salad
- Make katsu sauce
- Make meatballs
  (if using homemade)

UP TO 1 DAY

- Bread chicken for katsu
- Thaw meatballs in refrigerator

PREP AHEAD

- Peel and trim parsnips
- Zest and juice 3 lemons
- Mince celery
- Shred carrots
- Grate onion
- Mix katsu sauce
- Break broccoli into florets
- Cube zucchini

GROCERY LIST

PROTEIN

- Bone-in, skin-on chicken thighs 12 (about 4 pounds total)
- Boneless, skinless chicken breasts 3 (about 1½ pounds total)
- Ground chicken 4 pounds

PRODUCE

- Broccoli 1 head
- Broccoli slaw 1 (9-ounce) package
- Celery stalk 1
- Dill 1 bunch
- Fresh oregano and dill for garnishing
- Fresh parsley for serving
- Large carrots 2
- Lemons 3
- Medium yellow onion 1
- Oregano 2 small bunches
- Parsnips 3 pounds
- Zucchini 2

REFRIGERATOR

- Crumbled dairy-free feta cheese for garnishing
- Dairy-free Parmesan cheese for serving
- Dairy-free plain yogurt for garnishing
- Eggs 2

FREEZER

- Frozen meatballs (see page 34; cooked or uncooked, chicken or beef) 2 pounds
- Cauliflower rice for serving

CUPBOARD & COUNTER

- Apple cider vinegar 1 tablespoon
- Arrowroot powder ½ cup
- Artichoke hearts, packed in water 2 (14-ounce) cans
- Avocado oil mayonnaise 1 cup
- Coconut aminos 2¼ cups
- Fish sauce 3½ tablespoons
- Garlic powder ¾ teaspoon
- Grain-free elbow macaroni 1 (8-ounce) box
- Grain-free fusilli or penne pasta 3 (8-ounce) boxes
- Healthy in a Hurry Mediterranean Seasoning (page 37) 1½ teaspoons
- Honey ⅓ cup
- Italian seasoning 1 teaspoon
- Marinara sauce 1 (32-ounce) jar
- Pitted green olives for garnishing
- Pork rind crumbs 1 cup
- Toasted sesame oil 2 tablespoons plus 2 teaspoons
- Unsalted chicken bone broth 4 cups
- Unseasoned rice vinegar 1 tablespoon, or 1½ teaspoons apple cider vinegar
- Unsweetened ketchup ½ cup
- White pepper 2 teaspoons
- White wine vinegar 1 teaspoon

Greek Lemon Chicken
with Artichokes

3 pounds parsnips, peeled and thin ends discarded

12 bone-in, skin-on chicken thighs (about 4 pounds total)

3 lemons

½ cup extra-virgin olive oil

1 tablespoon sea salt

1½ teaspoons Healthy in a Hurry Mediterranean Seasoning (page 37)

2 small bunches oregano

1 bunch dill

2 (14-ounce) cans artichoke hearts, packed in water, drained

Cracked black pepper, fresh oregano and dill, pitted green olives, dairy-free plain yogurt, and crumbled dairy-free feta cheese for garnishing

PREP AHEAD

Peel and trim parsnips

Zest and juice lemons

MAKE AHEAD

Refrigerate, uncooked, up to 3 days; cooked, up to 1 week

Freeze up to 4 months

NOTES AND SHORTCUTS

Substitute baby Yukon gold potatoes for parsnips

Sub Italian seasoning for Mediterranean

Sub pitted green olives for artichokes

Parsnips that are 1 to 2 inches thick will cook evenly and fit well in the freezer; halve larger ones lengthwise

Make one batch to cook now and a second batch to freeze for later.

Divide parsnips equally between your cooking pot (Instant Pot, slow cooker, or baking sheet) and a 9-inch glass container or freezer bag. Divide chicken and place on top of parsnips. Finely grate zest and juice lemons over chicken in cooking pot and freezer container. Equally divide oil, salt, Mediterranean seasoning, oregano, and dill between each container, then distribute artichoke hearts on top. Seal freezer container and store in freezer for later.

TO COOK NOW

Instant Pot: Secure lid and set pressure valve to seal. Cook on high pressure with a 10-minute timer. Let pressure release naturally for 7 minutes. Quick-release any remaining pressure.

Slow Cooker: Add ½ cup water and cook on low for 8 hours or high for 4 hours.

Discard herbs and skin, if desired, then divide chicken and parsnips among serving bowls. Pour cooking liquid through a fine-mesh strainer, then spoon liquid over bowls. Garnish with black pepper, fresh herbs, olives, yogurt, and feta cheese, if desired, before serving.

TO COOK LATER

Instant Pot: Remove container from freezer and allow to thaw just enough to remove contents. Cook as directed above but with a 20-minute timer.

Slow Cooker: Remove container from freezer and allow to thaw completely. Cook as directed above.

12

PREP AHEAD

Mince celery

Shred carrots

Grate onion

Mix sauce

MAKE AHEAD

Refrigerate mac salad
up to 10 days and
sauce up to 2 weeks

Refrigerate chicken up to
5 days. Reheat on a cooling
rack at 450°F for 3 to
5 minutes.

TIPS AND SHORTCUTS

Use any grain- or gluten-
free elbow pasta. See
note on page 118 if using
cassava pasta.

Sub peeled and cubed sweet
potatoes or celeriac for
pasta; boil until fork-tender

Sub ground plantain chips
for pork rind crumbs or
grain- and gluten-free panko
bread crumbs; look for Jeff
Nathan Creations brand

Want a super-simple
shortcut? Purchase your
favorite brand of grain-
free or gluten-free chicken
tenders and use them
in place of the breaded
chicken.

Chicken Katsu with Mac Salad

MAC SALAD

1 (8-ounce) box grain-free elbow
macaroni

1 cup avocado oil mayonnaise

1 tablespoon apple cider vinegar

1 tablespoon honey

½ teaspoon sea salt

¼ teaspoon cracked black pepper

1 celery stalk, minced

2 large carrots, shredded

¼ medium yellow onion, grated

KATSU SAUCE

½ cup unsweetened ketchup

¼ cup honey

3 tablespoons coconut aminos

1 teaspoon white wine vinegar

2 teaspoons fish sauce

½ teaspoon garlic powder

CHICKEN

1 cup pork rind crumbs

¼ teaspoon garlic powder

Sea salt and ground white pepper

2 eggs

¼ cup arrowroot powder

3 boneless, skinless chicken
breasts (1½ pounds total),
sliced in half lengthwise to
make 6 cutlets

½ cup avocado oil, plus more
for spritzing

To make salad: Fill a large saucepan with salted water and bring
to a boil. Stir in macaroni and cook for 1 minute less than package
direction states.

In a large bowl, combine mayonnaise, vinegar, honey, salt, and black
pepper to make a dressing.

Drain macaroni and rinse with cold water.

Add macaroni, celery, carrots, and onion to dressing and mix to
combine. Cover and refrigerate salad while preparing the chicken
and sauce. Remix before serving.

To make sauce: In a small jar, stir together ketchup, honey, coconut
aminos, vinegar, fish sauce, and garlic powder. Set aside.

To make chicken: In a shallow bowl, stir together pork rind crumbs,
garlic powder, 1 teaspoon salt, and ¼ teaspoon white pepper. In a
second shallow bowl, beat eggs. Add arrowroot powder to a third bowl.

Season chicken cutlets on both sides with salt and white pepper.
Coat chicken in arrowroot powder, shaking off excess, then dip each
cutlet into egg, then press each into pork rind crumbs, until all are
well coated on both sides.

Line a large plate with paper towels.

In a large skillet over medium heat, warm ¼ cup oil until it shimmers. Add four cutlets and pan-fry until golden brown, 3 to 4 minutes per side. Transfer to prepared plate to drain.

Drain used oil from skillet and add remaining ¼ cup oil. Repeat with remaining two cutlets.

Preheat oven to 450°F. Lightly grease a cooling rack and set over a baking sheet.

Lay cutlets on prepared rack and spritz with oil. Bake for 15 minutes, until breading is golden and chicken is cooked through. Slice chicken into strips and drizzle sauce over top.

Serve with mac salad alongside.

12

SERVES 6 TO 8
ACTIVE TIME: 12 MINUTES

PREP AHEAD

Make sauce

Cube zucchini

Break broccoli into florets

MAKE AHEAD

Refrigerate up to 5 days

Freeze up to 4 months

NOTES AND SHORTCUTS

Substitute any vegetables you have left over in your crisper; asparagus, mushrooms, green beans, sugar snap peas, bell peppers, and cauliflower will all work

Substitute leftover shredded chicken, shrimp, or ground pork for ground chicken

Fridge Clean-Out Stir-Fry Chicken

1 tablespoon avocado oil

4 pounds ground chicken

1 (9-ounce) package broccoli slaw

¾ cup Stir-Fry Sauce (recipe below)

2 tablespoons arrowroot powder (optional)

2 zucchini, quartered lengthwise and cut into 1-inch cubes

1 head broccoli, cut into small florets

Cauliflower rice for serving

In a large skillet over medium-high heat, warm oil until it shimmers. Add chicken and cook for 5 to 7 minutes, until well browned all over. Stir in broccoli slaw and sauté for 2 to 3 minutes, until tender.

In a small bowl, combine stir-fry sauce and arrowroot powder (if using) and whisk to make a slurry. Pour slurry into skillet, stir to mix, turn heat to high, and bring sauce to a boil. Boil for 1 to 2 minutes, until thickened. Add zucchini and broccoli, remove skillet from heat, cover, and let steam for 3 to 5 minutes, until vegetables are crisp-tender.

Serve hot, over cauliflower rice.

Stir-Fry Sauce

MAKES 2½ CUPS

2 cups coconut aminos

2 tablespoons plus 2 teaspoons fish sauce

2 tablespoons plus 2 teaspoons toasted sesame oil

1 tablespoon unseasoned rice vinegar, or 1½ teaspoons apple cider vinegar

1½ teaspoons fine sea salt

1 teaspoon ground white pepper

In a large jar, combine the coconut aminos, fish sauce, sesame oil, vinegar, salt, and white pepper. Cap tightly and shake vigorously to mix. Store in refrigerator for 3 months.

Magic Meatball Pasta

2 tablespoons extra-virgin olive oil

2 pounds frozen meatballs (see page 34; cooked or uncooked, chicken or beef)

1½ teaspoons sea salt

1 teaspoon Italian seasoning

3 (8-ounce) boxes grain-free fusilli or penne pasta

1 (32-ounce) jar marinara sauce

4 cups unsalted chicken bone broth

Dairy-free Parmesan cheese and chopped parsley for serving

Instant Pot: Add oil to an Instant Pot and turn to sauté mode on high. Add meatballs, salt, and Italian seasoning. Stir to combine. (The meatballs will be browned slightly but not defrosted or cooked through.) Add pasta over top. Without stirring, spoon sauce over noodles and then broth.

Secure lid and set valve to seal. Cook on high pressure with a 4-minute timer with a quick release. Remove lid and stir pasta well. Remove pot from base so pasta doesn't overcook. There will be some extra sauce at top, but as you stir, pasta will continue cooking and absorb some liquid. If needed to thicken, switch pot back to sauté mode for 30 to 60 seconds, until sauce has reduced.

Stovetop: In a large Dutch oven with a tight-fitting lid over medium-high heat, add ingredients as listed above. Ensure noodles are fully submerged in the broth. Bring mixture to a boil over medium-high heat, then reduce heat to low. Cover pot with lid and let mixture simmer for 14 to 17 minutes, until noodles are tender. Stir occasionally to prevent sticking.

Serve hot, topped with Parmesan and parsley.

12

SERVES 6 TO 8
ACTIVE TIME: 12 MINUTES

MAKE AHEAD

Refrigerate pasta up to 3 days; to reheat, add ¼ to ½ cup broth and gently heat in a skillet over medium-low heat

Make meatballs up to 4 months

NOTES AND SHORTCUTS

Store-bought meatball brands: Amylu Foods, Aidells, Cooked Perfect, Sprouts, Trader Joe's

Sub sliced sausages for meatballs

This recipe was tested using cassava pasta, which absorbs more liquid and cooks more quickly than most. For other types of dried pasta, such as chickpea, lentil, or brown rice pasta, set Instant Pot timer for half of time called for on box, minus 1 minute. So, if your box calls for 12 minutes, set it for 5 minutes; if 8 minutes, cook for 3 minutes.

Don't walk away for more than 5 minutes after timer has finished. Your pasta will overcook.

Use frozen meatballs! This not only makes everything so much easier and saves time, but it helps meatballs keep their shape and not break apart in pot or stick to bottom. Uncooked or cooked, both take the same amount of time.

Week 13

13

This is a prep day, doing double duty as a weekly meal plan. The grilled chicken reintroduces you to my beloved green goddess dressing, the superstar you encountered in Week 4 (page 83). This dressing works as both a marinade and a sauce, infusing your chicken with exquisite flavor. And bonus: you'll use it again at the tail end of the week.

Your week is streamlined with the help of a rotisserie chicken for a Greek-style soup with the silky and lemony notes reminiscent of avgolemono soup but without the starchy rice.

I think the Cuban-inspired picadillo will become a family favorite. It's a delightful nod to Latin beef stew but prepared in half the time.

Finally, we end the week with a hearty Cobb salad that makes efficient use of both the green goddess dressing and the rotisserie chicken introduced earlier. The crispy chicken-skin croutons add a grain-free crunch to this salad.

MAKE AHEAD

UP TO 1 WEEK
- Make green goddess dressing

UP TO 3 DAYS
- Shred rotisserie chicken for Cobb salad
- Cook and chop bacon for Cobb salad
- Hard-boil eggs for Cobb salad

UP TO 2 DAYS
- Marinate chicken in green goddess dressing for grilled chicken

PREP AHEAD
- Slice radishes; store in cold water
- Separate egg yolks
- Juice 2 lemons
- Chop dill
- Mince 2 onions
- Mince 8 garlic cloves
- Dice bell pepper
- Mix spices for picadillo
- Slice red onion
- Halve cherry tomatoes

GROCERY LIST

PROTEIN

- Boneless, skinless chicken thighs 2 pounds
- Ground beef 2 pounds
- Rotisserie chicken 1
- Sugar- and nitrate-free bacon 6 slices

PRODUCE

- Avocados 2
- Cherry tomatoes 1 pint
- Fresh cilantro 1 small bunch
- Fresh dill 1 bunch
- Fresh lemon juice ⅓ cup
- Fresh oregano for serving
- Garlic cloves 8
- Green bell pepper 1
- Lemons 2
- Little Gem lettuce 4 cups
- Medium yellow onions 2
- Pea shoot tendrils or other microgreens 1 cup
- Radishes 1 small bunch
- Small potatoes 6
- Small red onion 1

REFRIGERATOR

- Crumbled dairy-free feta cheese ¼ cup
- Egg yolks 3
- Green Goddess Dressing (page 83) 1⅓ cups
- Hard-boiled eggs 4

FREEZER

- Cauliflower rice for serving
- Frozen cauliflower rice 1 (12-ounce) package

CUPBOARD & COUNTER

- Arrowroot powder 1½ tablespoons
- Bay leaves 2
- Crushed tomatoes 2 (14- to 18-ounce) jars or boxes
- Golden raisins 1 cup
- Ground cinnamon 1 teaspoon
- Ground cumin 2 tablespoons
- Plantain tostones for serving
- Red wine vinegar 3 tablespoons
- Unsalted chicken bone broth 6 cups
- Whole pitted green olives 1 (10-ounce) jar

13

PREP AHEAD

Marinate chicken in refrigerator up to 48 hours for more flavor

Make sauce up to 2 weeks in advance

Slice radishes; store in cold water

MAKE AHEAD

Marinate and freeze chicken up to 6 months; defrost overnight in refrigerator and cook according to directions at right

Refrigerate grilled chicken, herbs stored separately, up to 1 week

NOTES AND SHORTCUTS

Use Violife dairy-free feta or sheep's milk feta if dairy is tolerated

Sauce works as marinade for shrimp or fish when grilling as well; decrease marinating time to 20 minutes

Green Goddess Grilled Chicken with Feta and Cilantro

1 cup Green Goddess Dressing (page 83)

2 pounds boneless, skinless chicken thighs

Sea salt and cracked black pepper

¼ cup crumbled dairy-free feta cheese

1 small bunch cilantro leaves and tender stems

1 small bunch radishes, stems removed and thinly sliced

Lemon wedges for serving

In a shallow dish, combine ½ cup sauce and chicken and toss to coat. Transfer to refrigerator and let marinate for 6 hours.

Prepare a grill for medium heat. Discard marinade and scrape any excess from chicken, then season generously with salt and pepper.

Grill chicken for 3 to 4 minutes per side, until an instant-read thermometer inserted into middle of a thigh registers 165°F. Arrange chicken on a platter and top with feta, cilantro, and radishes.

Serve with lemon wedges and remaining sauce for dipping.

Greek Lemon-Chicken Soup

6 cups unsalted chicken bone broth

1 (12-ounce) package frozen cauliflower rice

1½ tablespoons arrowroot powder

3 egg yolks

⅓ cup fresh lemon juice

2 cups shredded rotisserie chicken

¼ cup packed chopped dill, plus more for garnishing

2½ teaspoons sea salt

¼ teaspoon cracked black pepper

In a blender, combine broth, half of cauliflower rice, and arrowroot and puree on high speed for 30 seconds, until smooth. Pour into a large stockpot and bring to a boil. Turn heat to medium and let simmer for 5 to 7 minutes until thickened.

In a small bowl, whisk together egg yolks and lemon juice until frothy. Slowly pour one ladle of hot broth mixture into egg mixture, while whisking constantly, to temper egg yolks so they don't curdle on stove. Add egg mixture to pot and stir to incorporate. Stir in chicken, remaining half of cauliflower rice, dill, and salt and black pepper.

Serve hot.

SERVES 4
ACTIVE TIME: 20 MINUTES

PREP AHEAD

Separate egg yolks

Shred chicken

Juice lemons

Chop dill

MAKE AHEAD

Refrigerate up to 5 days

Freeze up to 4 months

NOTES AND SHORTCUTS

To make starch-free, substitute ⅓ cup unsalted raw cashew pieces for arrowroot; blend into broth with cauliflower

13

PREP AHEAD

Mince onions

Dice green pepper

Press garlic

Mix spices

MAKE AHEAD

Refrigerate up to 1 week

Freeze up to 3 months

NOTES AND SHORTCUTS

Chop onions, garlic, and bell pepper in a food processor

Sub Thompson raisins for golden

Trader Joe's and Whole Foods carry ready-made tostones

In a pinch, I love to cut open a bag of Whole Food Pilaf-Style Riced Cauliflower for this recipe. I sauté it in a dry pan over medium heat until defrosted and heated through, 3 to 5 minutes.

Cuban-Inspired Picadillo with Crispy Plantain Tostones

2 tablespoons avocado oil

2 medium yellow onions, minced

1 green bell pepper, seeded and diced

8 garlic cloves, crushed with a garlic press

2 pounds ground beef

2 tablespoons ground cumin

1 teaspoon ground cinnamon

2 bay leaves

6 small potatoes, peeled and cubed

2 (14- to 18-ounce) jars or boxes crushed tomatoes

3 tablespoons red wine vinegar

¾ teaspoon sea salt

¼ teaspoon cracked black pepper

1 (10-ounce) jar whole pitted green olives, drained

1 cup golden raisins

Cauliflower rice, fresh oregano, and plantain tostones for serving

In a large cast-iron skillet over medium-high heat, warm oil until it shimmers. Add onions, bell pepper, and garlic and sauté for 8 to 10 minutes, until onions have softened. Add beef and brown well, breaking up pieces with a wooden spoon. Stir in cumin, cinnamon, bay leaves, potatoes, tomatoes, vinegar, salt, and black pepper.

Turn heat to low, cover, and let simmer for 20 minutes, until potatoes are fork-tender and liquid has mostly evaporated. Uncover and stir in olives and raisins and continue to simmer for 10 to 15 minutes longer, until potatoes are tender and sauce has thickened.

Serve hot, over cauliflower rice, sprinkled with oregano leaves, with tostones alongside.

Green Goddess Cobb Salad with Crispy Chicken-Skin Croutons

SERVES 4 TO 6
ACTIVE TIME: 20 MINUTES

6 slices sugar- and nitrate-free bacon

2 cups shredded rotisserie chicken, skin removed and reserved

4 cups Little Gem lettuce, torn if large

1 cup pea shoot tendrils or other microgreens

½ small red onion, thinly sliced

4 hard-boiled eggs, chopped

1 pint cherry tomatoes, halved

2 avocados, cut into ¼-inch slices

⅓ cup Green Goddess Dressing (page 83)

Line a plate with paper towels.

In a medium skillet over medium heat, cook bacon, flipping halfway through, until fat is rendered and bacon is crisp, 5 to 7 minutes. Using tongs, transfer bacon to prepared plate to drain, leaving grease in pan.

Add chicken skin to bacon grease, turn heat to low, and cook, turning and pressing occasionally, until skin is golden brown and crisp, 5 to 7 minutes. Meanwhile, chop bacon.

Transfer skins to prepared plate to drain.

Layer all components in a large bowl. Drizzle with dressing and toss to combine before serving.

PREP AHEAD

Cook and chop bacon

Shred chicken

Slice onion

Hard-boil eggs

Halve cherry tomatoes

MAKE AHEAD

Refrigerate dressing up to 2 weeks

Refrigerate salad up to 5 days. Layer dressing evenly in bottom of one large or four smaller containers; add everything but crispy chicken skins and avocados and seal tightly.

NOTES AND SHORTCUTS

Poach fresh chicken if you do not have rotisserie chicken or leftover chicken. Fill a small pot halfway with water and bring to a boil. Add 1 pound boneless, skinless chicken breasts, turn heat to low, partially cover pot, and simmer for 8 minutes. Remove pot from heat and let chicken sit in hot water, covered, for 15 minutes. Remove chicken from pot, allow to cool, then dice or shred.

Week 14

14

This week shows you that with a bit of foresight and a few shortcuts, you can enjoy a delicious and varied menu that's easy to execute.

We start with a simple and flavor-packed shredded chicken to use in tacos. Make two batches—one for a delicious dinner complete with taco fixings and another to repurpose in the skillet hash. Any chicken that remains can be used in the Beef and Zucchini Enchiladas Verdes (page 163).

The lettuce wraps are inspired by a Greek dish typically served in pitas with vegetables and a yogurt-based tzatziki sauce. It can also serve double duty if you double up on the ingredients during your grocery run. Freeze the prepared chicken for up to six months, then pull it out to grill and pair with a simple salad tossed with one of my marinades (see page 246). You'll need a lot of chicken this week, so buy it on sale if you can.

As the week unfolds, you'll really appreciate the convenience of the make-ahead options. Marinate the steak for the lettuce cups up to two days or marinate them and freeze for later use. The sauce, a true powerhouse, will last for weeks and is equally amazing on salads.

MAKE AHEAD

UP TO 1 WEEK
- Make tinga sauce
- Make tzatziki for lettuce cups
- Make Thai sauce for lettuce cups

UP TO 5 DAYS
- Make soft-boiled eggs for hash

UP TO 3 DAYS
- Marinate chicken for souvlaki

UP TO 2 DAYS
- Marinate steak

PREP AHEAD

- Quarter 2 yellow onions
- Peel garlic, mince 2 cloves
- Slice tomatoes and red onion
- Shred potatoes, if making homemade
- Chop cilantro
- Zest and juice 2 lemons
- Juice 3 limes
- Chop cashews
- Washed and separate butter lettuce
- Julienne bell pepper

GROCERY LIST

PROTEIN

- Boneless, skinless chicken thighs 9 pounds
- Grass-fed skirt steak 1 ½ pounds

PRODUCE

- Avocado 3, for serving
- Baby spinach 1 (5-ounce) package
- Butter lettuce 1 head
- Diced red onion for serving
- Fresh cilantro 2 small bunches
- Fresh mint 1 small bunch
- Garlic cloves 10 (about 1 head)
- Lemons 2
- Limes 2
- Persian cucumber 1
- Red bell pepper 1
- Roma tomatoes 2, for serving
- Small yellow onions 2
- Tricolor slaw mix 1 (8-ounce) package

REFRIGERATOR

- Dairy-free ranch dressing ¼ cup
- Eggs 4
- Grain-free tortillas or butter lettuce 12 for serving
- Plain unsweetened dairy-free thick yogurt 1 cup

FREEZER

- Frozen shredded hash browns 2 (12-ounce) packages

CUPBOARD & COUNTER

- Apple cider vinegar 1 ½ teaspoons
- Cayenne pepper ½ teaspoon
- Coconut aminos 2 tablespoons
- Diced tomatoes 4 (14-ounce) jars or cans
- Dry roasted cashews ¼ cup
- Ground chipotle powder 2 teaspoons
- Ground ginger ½ teaspoon
- Healthy in a Hurry Mediterranean Seasoning (page 37) 2 tablespoons
- Healthy in a Hurry Taco Seasoning (page 37) 2 tablespoons
- Honey 1 tablespoon
- Hot sauce optional topping
- Pickled jalapeños optional topping
- Pure maple syrup 1 tablespoon
- Salsa of your choice optional topping
- Sweet paprika 2 teaspoons
- Toasted sesame oil 1 teaspoon
- Unsweetened almond butter 2 tablespoons

14

SERVES 6 NOW, 6 LATER
ACTIVE TIME: 35 MINUTES

PREP AHEAD

Quarter onions

Make sauce

MAKE AHEAD

Refrigerate sauce
up to 3 weeks

Refrigerate mixture,
uncooked, up to 3 days;
cooked, up to 1 week

Freeze, cooked, up to
4 months; uncooked,
up to 6 months

NOTES AND SHORTCUTS

Sub any taco seasoning
for my specialty blend

Sub ancho chile powder
for chipotle powder

Sub cubed pork tenderloin
or stew meat for chicken

Chicken Tinga

6 tablespoons avocado oil

2 small yellow onions, quartered

8 garlic cloves

2 tablespoons Healthy in a Hurry
Taco Seasoning (page 37)

2 teaspoons ground
chipotle powder

4 (14-ounce) jars or cans
diced tomatoes

3 teaspoons sea salt

6 pounds boneless, skinless
chicken thighs

12 warmed grain-free tortillas
or butter lettuce for serving

Avocado slices, diced red onion,
and cilantro leaves for serving

Make one batch to cook now and a second batch to refrigerate
for the Taco Skillet Hash (page 210) or to freeze for later.

In a blender, combine oil, onions, garlic, taco seasoning, chipotle
powder, tomatoes, and salt and puree until smooth.

Equally divide chicken thighs between your cooking pot (Instant Pot
or slow cooker) and a 9-inch glass container or freezer bag. Pour
half of blended sauce into each container. Seal freezer container
and store in freezer for later.

TO COOK NOW

Instant Pot: Secure lid and set valve to seal. Cook on high
pressure with a 12-minute timer. Let pressure release naturally for
15 minutes. Quick-release any remaining pressure.

Slow Cooker: Cook on low for 6 hours or high for 3 hours.

Shred chicken and serve in warmed tortillas with avocado, onion,
and cilantro.

TO COOK LATER

Instant Pot: Remove container from freezer and allow to thaw just
enough to remove contents. Place in Instant pot with ¼ cup water.
Cook as directed above but use a 30-minute timer.

Slow Cooker: Remove container from freezer and allow to thaw
completely. Cook as directed above.

Chicken Souvlaki Lettuce Wraps

14

SERVES 4 TO 6
ACTIVE TIME: 25 MINUTES
(PLUS 3 HOURS'
MARINATING TIME)

TZATZIKI

1 small Persian cucumber, halved, seeded, and finely chopped

1 cup plain unsweetened dairy-free thick yogurt

1 small bunch mint, finely chopped

1 garlic clove, crushed with a garlic press

Juice of 1 lemon

1 pinch sea salt

¼ cup extra-virgin olive oil, plus more for brushing

2 tablespoons Healthy in a Hurry Mediterranean Seasoning (page 37)

2 teaspoons sweet paprika

Zest and juice of 1 lemon

Sea salt and cracked black pepper

3 pounds boneless, skinless chicken thighs

Butter lettuce cups, thinly sliced Roma tomatoes, thinly sliced red onion, and fresh herbs, such as dill and mint, for serving

PREP AHEAD

Marinate chicken in refrigerator up to 3 days or freeze up to 6 months; defrost in refrigerator overnight

---

MAKE AHEAD

Refrigerate tzatziki up to 10 days

NOTES AND SHORTCUTS

Dairy-free yogurt brands: Cocojune and Culina work best for this

Purchase store-bought tzatziki such as Kite Hill

To make tzatziki: In a small bowl, mix together cucumber, yogurt, mint, garlic, lemon juice, and salt. Refrigerate until ready to serve.

In a small bowl, combine oil, Mediterranean seasoning, paprika, lemon zest and juice, and a generous pinch of salt and black pepper and mix into a marinade. Place chicken in a large resealable plastic bag and add marinade. Seal and mix well, ensuring each thigh is coated. Refrigerate for 3 hours.

Heat broiler to its highest level with oven rack placed one rung down from top. Set a cooling rack on a baking sheet.

Remove chicken from fridge and discard marinade. Arrange chicken in a single layer on prepared rack. Place baking sheet under hot broiler and cook chicken for 15 to 20 minutes, regularly brushing with oil and any juices from bottom of pan; flip chicken halfway through cooking. Once cooked, remove pan from oven and let chicken rest for 5 minutes. Coarsely chop chicken.

Serve in lettuce cups with tomatoes, red onion, tzatziki, and herbs.

14

SERVES 4
ACTIVE TIME: 15 MINUTES

PREP AHEAD

Shred potatoes, if making homemade

Chop cilantro

Slice avocado

MAKE AHEAD

Refrigerate hash up to 5 days

Cook eggs fresh before serving or use Instant Pot Soft-Boiled Eggs (page 253)

NOTES AND SHORTCUTS

Cascadian Farm sells an organic blend of shredded frozen potatoes, carrots, and sweet potatoes that works wonderfully here, as will 1 pound of potatoes, peeled and grated with a food processor or box grater

Sub 2 cups rotisserie chicken plus 1 tablespoon Healthy in a Hurry Taco Seasoning (page 37) for taco chicken

Sub Shredded Carnitas Pork (page 104) for taco chicken

Make vegetarian by sautéing chopped zucchini and bell peppers in place of chicken tinga

Taco Skillet Hash

2 tablespoons avocado oil, plus more for drizzling

2 (12-ounce) packages frozen shredded hash browns, thawed

1½ cups Chicken Tinga (page 206)

4 eggs

1 (5-ounce) package baby spinach

1 small bunch cilantro, tender stems and leaves chopped

¼ cup dairy-free ranch dressing

Sliced avocado, salsa, pickled jalapeños, and hot sauce for serving (optional)

In a large skillet over medium-high heat, warm oil until it shimmers. Add hash browns and pan-fry for 5 to 7 minutes, until crispy. Transfer to a plate and set aside.

Add chicken to skillet and cook for 3 to 5 minutes, until heated through, stirring occasionally. Push meat to side of skillet and add a drizzle of oil. Gently crack eggs in one at a time and fry for 2 to 3 minutes, until whites are set and yolks are runny. Transfer eggs to a plate and return hash browns to skillet along with spinach. Stir together, then remove from heat.

Add eggs back to skillet and top with cilantro and a drizzle of ranch dressing. Serve with avocado, salsa, pickled jalapeños, and hot sauce alongside, if desired.

Thai Steak Lettuce Cups

ALMOND SAUCE

2 tablespoons unsweetened almond butter

1 tablespoon pure maple syrup

1 garlic clove, crushed with a garlic press

Juice of 1 small lime

1½ teaspoons apple cider vinegar

1 teaspoon toasted sesame oil

½ teaspoon ground ginger

½ teaspoon cayenne pepper

¼ teaspoon sea salt

⅓ cup extra-virgin olive oil

1½ pounds grass-fed skirt steak

2 tablespoons coconut aminos

1 tablespoon honey

½ tablespoon lime juice

Sea salt and cracked black pepper

1 head butter lettuce, washed and separated into leaves

1 (8-ounce) package tricolor slaw mix

1 red bell pepper, seeded and julienned

¼ cup packed cilantro leaves and stems

¼ cup dry roasted cashews, chopped

SERVES 4 TO 6
ACTIVE TIME: 35 MINUTES
(PLUS 4 HOURS' MARINATING TIME)

PREP AHEAD

Prepare sauce

Wash and separate butter lettuce

Seed and julienne bell pepper

Marinate steak in fridge up to 2 days

MAKE AHEAD

Refrigerate, components stored separately, up to 1 week

Refrigerate sauce up to 1 month

NOTES AND SHORTCUTS

Tricolor slaw mixes consist of both red and green cabbage and shredded carrots; to make your own, purchase individual vegetables and shred them

Sub napa cabbage for slaw mix

Sub Ginger-Sesame Dressing (page 33) for sauce

Sub shrimp or chicken for steak

Sub mint or basil for cilantro

To make sauce: In a small bowl, whisk together almond butter, maple syrup, garlic, lime juice, vinegar, sesame oil, ginger, cayenne, and salt. Gradually whisk in olive oil. If needed, whisk in 1 to 2 tablespoons water to thin.

Place steak in a large non-reactive bowl and add ¼ cup sauce, coconut aminos, honey, and lime juice. Toss to coat, then cover and let marinate in refrigerator for 4 hours. Refrigerate remaining sauce.

Preheat a grill for medium heat.

Remove steak from marinade and season generously with salt and black pepper. Grill for 3 to 4 minutes per side, depending on thickness of steak. Remove steak from grill and let rest, uncovered, on a plate for 5 minutes. Transfer to a cutting board and slice against grain into thin strips.

Serve with lettuce cups, slaw, bell pepper, cilantro, cashews, and remaining sauce.

Week 15

We begin the week by making a batch of my versatile nacho sauce, which is delightfully cheese-free yet packed with veggies. If you've been part of my community for any amount of time, you've likely encountered the magic of this sauce, known as skillet queso, cheesy nacho sauce, or simply queso. Its sorcery transcends dietary preferences, appealing to junk food aficionados and health-conscious eaters alike. Beyond just a dipping sauce, it moonlights as a silky pasta companion in my Tex-Mex Mac and Cheese (see page 224).

Next up: shrimp and spaghetti squash drenched in a creamy sauce made with feta and tomatoes. It's made in one pan and works well as a make-ahead meal; just add the fresh shrimp as you reheat.

For this week's Sheet-Pan Smashed Potato Nachos, sub in Shredded Carnitas Pork (page 104) or ground beef taco meat for the chicken tinga if you ate it all or haven't done Meal Plan 14 yet.

My mac and cheese tastes like the one from my childhood: It's a comforting and creamy one-pot dinner that promises to satisfy your cravings with its cheesy and zesty sauce.

And my Cajun salmon shines with a vibrant salsa and coconut rice. If you want to skip a step, purchase your favorite salsa from the store.

MAKE AHEAD

UP TO 1 WEEK

- Make nacho sauce
- Roast spaghetti squash and make tomato sauce
- Brown and drain ground beef for mac and cheese
- Make coconut-lime rice

UP TO 3 DAYS

- Boil potatoes for nachos
- Season salmon
- Make salsa for Cajun salmon
- Thaw taco chicken, if frozen

UP TO 2 DAYS

- Add all ingredients for mac and cheese to Instant Pot insert. Cover and refrigerate.

PREP AHEAD

- Mince 1 head garlic
- Chop mango, cilantro, and pineapple
- Mince jalapeño and red onion
- Shred lettuce
- Juice 2 limes
- Juice lemon
- Dice tomatoes

GROCERY LIST

PROTEIN

- Ground beef ½ pound
- Medium wild-caught shrimp, peeled and deveined 1½ pounds
- Wild-caught salmon 2 pounds

PRODUCE

- Avocado optional topping
- Baby creamer potatoes or white-fleshed sweet potatoes 2 pounds
- Carrots ¾ pound
- Cherry tomatoes 1 pint
- Diced fresh pineapple 1 cup
- Diced tomatoes optional topping
- Fresh basil 1 bunch
- Fresh cilantro 1 bunch
- Garlic cloves 12 (about 1 head)
- Jalapeño 1
- Lemon 1
- Limes 2
- Mango 1
- Red onion 1
- Shredded lettuce optional topping
- Spaghetti squash 1 (3-pound)
- White-fleshed sweet potatoes 1½ pounds

REFRIGERATOR

- Dairy-free feta cheese 1 cup
- Dairy-free sour cream for serving (optional)
- Guacamole for serving (optional)

FREEZER

- Frozen cauliflower rice 2 (12-ounce) bags
- Chicken Tinga 1 cup (page 206)

CUPBOARD & COUNTER

- Arrowroot powder ¼ cup
- Coconut oil 2 teaspoons
- Dried grain-free elbow macaroni 12 ounces
- Full-fat coconut milk ¼ cup
- Ghee ⅔ cup plus 3 tablespoons
- Healthy in a Hurry Cajun Seasoning (page 37) 1½ teaspoons
- Healthy in a Hurry Taco Seasoning (page 37) 3½ tablespoons
- Honey 2 teaspoons
- Mild roasted tomatillo salsa 1 cup
- Nutritional yeast ¼ cup
- Pickled jalapeños ⅓ cup, plus more as optional topping
- Salsa of your choice 1 cup
- Tomato paste 2 tablespoons
- Unsalted beef bone broth 2 cups (16 ounces)
- Unsalted chicken bone broth 5 cups

15

MAKES 12 CUPS
ACTIVE TIME: 20 MINUTES

PREP AHEAD

Cube sweet potatoes

Dice carrots

MAKE AHEAD

Refrigerate up to 2 weeks or freeze up to 6 months.

NOTES AND SHORTCUTS

I use ghee for its buttery flavor, but it does have trace amounts of lactose and casein. To make this completely dairy-free, substitute your favorite vegan butter or use ½ cup avocado oil.

I choose white-fleshed sweet potato varieties because they are starchier and less sweet than traditional orange-fleshed yams, but any variety will work here.

Sub russet potatoes or parsnips for sweet potatoes and decrease broth by ¼ cup

Sub tapioca starch for arrowroot powder

Prep Recipe: Cheesy Nacho Sauce

1½ pounds white-fleshed sweet potatoes, peeled and cubed

¾ pound carrots, diced

5 cups unsalted chicken bone broth

⅔ cup ghee

¼ cup nutritional yeast

2 tablespoons fine sea salt

8 garlic cloves

1 cup mild roasted tomatillo salsa

¼ cup arrowroot powder

Combine sweet potatoes, carrots, broth, ghee, nutritional yeast, salt, garlic, and salsa in a saucepan. Bring to a boil over medium-high heat, then reduce heat to medium-low and cover. Simmer for 10 to 12 minutes, until tender.

In a blender, combine contents of pan and arrowroot powder and carefully blend on high speed until very smooth.

Return mixture to saucepan over medium-high heat and whisk constantly, about 5 minutes, until bubbling and thickened.

Transfer 4 cups sauce to a container and store in the refrigerator to use later this week. Ladle remaining sauce into two 12-cup silicone muffin molds, each holding ⅓ cup. Cover tightly and freeze, then pop out "pucks" (see page 20) into a resealable freezer bag. Remove pucks as needed (three pucks for 1 cup).

Shrimp and Spaghetti Squash with Feta-Tomato Sauce

1 (3-pound) spaghetti squash

4 tablespoons extra-virgin olive oil

Sea salt and cracked black pepper

1 pint cherry tomatoes

4 garlic cloves, minced

1 cup crumbled dairy-free feta cheese

1½ pounds medium wild-caught shrimp, peeled and deveined

½ cup chopped basil leaves

Juice of 1 lemon

PREP AHEAD

Mince garlic

Chop basil

MAKE AHEAD

Refrigerate roasted spaghetti squash and tomato sauce up to 1 week; add shrimp and bake just before serving.

NOTES AND SHORTCUTS

Sub shredded cooked chicken for shrimp

Dairy-free feta brands: Trader Joe's and Violife

Sub sheep's milk feta for dairy-free feta

Sub Kite Hill ricotta or Treeline "goat" cheese for feta

Sub parsley for basil

Place squash directly on middle rack of oven and turn temperature to 425°F. Once oven preheat timer goes off (about 10 minutes), carefully remove squash. This will soften squash enough to slice it.

Line a half sheet pan with parchment paper.

Once squash has cooled enough to handle, slice off both ends and cut crosswise into four or five rounds. Scoop out seeds from center of each round. Drizzle both sides of rounds with 1 tablespoon oil, then arrange in a single layer on prepared pan. Season with salt and pepper.

Place pan on middle rack in oven and bake for 15 minutes. In an 8-inch square baking dish, mix together tomatoes, garlic, feta, and remaining 3 tablespoons oil. Place dish in oven next to sheet pan and bake both for 15 minutes. Remove both pans from oven.

Using a fork, pull flesh from sides of squash rounds into noodle-like strands. Heap noodles onto pan; discard skins.

Stir shrimp into tomato mixture, return dish to oven, and bake for 2 to 3 minutes, until shrimp becomes pink. Remove dish from oven and season with salt and pepper. Add tomato mixture and shrimp to noodles, then sprinkle with basil and lemon juice.

Serve hot.

15

PREP AHEAD

Boil and drain potatoes

Thaw chicken tinga, if frozen

Thaw nacho sauce, if frozen

MAKE AHEAD

Refrigerate up to 5 days with toppings on side; warm under a broiler

NOTES AND SHORTCUTS

Sub 1 (11-ounce) bag of chips of your choice for potatoes

Sub avocado oil for ghee

Sub 2 cups shredded jack cheese for nacho sauce. Add with chicken to melt.

Sub ½ pound cooked ground meat, plus 2 teaspoons taco seasoning for chicken tinga

Sub ¼ cup plain dairy-free yogurt, such as Cocojune or Culina, mixed with 1 tablespoon fresh lime juice and ¼ teaspoon sea salt for dairy-free sour cream

Sheet-Pan Smashed-Potato Nachos

2 pounds baby creamer potatoes or cubed white-fleshed sweet potatoes

½ teaspoon coarse sea salt

3 tablespoons melted ghee

2 teaspoons Healthy in a Hurry Taco Seasoning (page 37)

¼ teaspoon cracked black pepper

1 cup Chicken Tinga (page 206), juices drained

1 cup Cheesy Nacho Sauce (page 218), warmed

⅓ cup pickled jalapeños

⅓ cup salsa

Dairy-free sour cream, guacamole, and fresh cilantro (optional)

Preheat oven to 450°F. Line a large sheet pan with parchment paper.

In a large pot over medium-high heat, combine potatoes and salt and add water to cover. Bring to a boil, then turn heat to low and let simmer for 15 minutes, until potatoes are fork-tender. Drain potatoes and add to prepared sheet pan.

Drizzle potatoes with ghee, then sprinkle with taco seasoning and black pepper and toss to coat. Using a heavy measuring cup or a drinking glass, firmly smash potatoes.

Roast potatoes until crisp, 20 to 25 minutes. Remove pan from oven and scatter shredded chicken over top. Turn oven temperature to broil and place pan on top rack. Broil for 2 to 3 minutes, until chicken is hot and potatoes are crisp.

Remove pan from oven and drizzle nacho sauce over top. Sprinkle with pickled jalapeños and salsa.

Serve with a dollop of sour cream and guacamole and a sprinkling of cilantro, if desired.

15

PREP AHEAD

Refrigerate nacho sauce up to 1 week or freeze up to 6 months; defrost 3 days in advance, if frozen

Add all ingredients to Instant Pot insert. Cover and refrigerate up to 2 days; bring to room temperature before pressure cooking.

MAKE AHEAD

Refrigerate up to 1 week

Freeze as a meal-prep kit up to 4 months: Brown and drain meat and add all ingredients except pasta to a resealable freezer bag or airtight container

Tex-Mex Mac and Cheese

½ pound ground beef

2 tablespoons tomato paste

3 tablespoons Healthy in a Hurry Taco Seasoning (page 37)

12 ounces dried grain-free elbow macaroni

2 cups unsalted beef bone broth

½ cup salsa

3 cups Cheesy Nacho Sauce (page 218)

Sliced avocado, shredded lettuce, diced tomatoes, pickled jalapeños, and cilantro for topping (optional)

In an Instant Pot on sauté mode set to high heat, brown ground beef. Drain grease, then stir in tomato paste and taco seasoning. Add pasta, broth, salsa, and nacho sauce, making sure pasta is all beneath liquid. Secure lid and set valve to seal. Cook on high pressure and with a 4-minute timer. Quick-release pressure, remove lid, and stir well.

Serve hot, topped with avocado, lettuce, tomatoes, jalapeños, and cilantro, if desired.

NOTES AND SHORTCUTS

Grain-free pasta, such as cassava or chickpea, typically comes in boxes that are 8 ounces, while gluten-free pasta, such as brown rice, lentil, or quinoa, typically comes in boxes that are 12 ounces. Use 1½ boxes of grain-free pasta or one whole box of gluten-free.

This recipe was tested with cassava pasta, which continues to cook and absorb liquid well after the timer. To use other pastas such as chickpea, lentil, or brown rice, set Instant Pot timer for half of time called for on box, minus 1 minute. So, if your box calls for 12 minutes, set timer for 5 minutes; if 8 minutes, cook for 3 minutes.

Nacho sauce can be added fresh or defrosted or as six frozen ⅓-cup "pucks" (see page 20); cook time will not change

Dairy-free queso brands: Siete, Trader Joe's organic vegan nacho dip, Core & Rind, Kite Hill

Cajun Salmon with Mango-Pineapple Salsa and Coconut-Lime Cauli Rice

2 pounds wild-caught salmon

2 teaspoons avocado oil

1½ teaspoons Healthy in a Hurry Cajun Seasoning (page 37)

1 pinch coarse sea salt

COCONUT-LIME CAULI RICE

2 teaspoons coconut oil

2 (12-ounce) bags frozen cauliflower rice

¼ cup chopped fresh cilantro leaves and tender stems

¼ cup full-fat coconut milk

1 tablespoon fresh lime juice

2 teaspoons honey

1 pinch sea salt

MANGO-PINEAPPLE SALSA

1 mango, diced

1 cup diced fresh pineapple

1 jalapeño, minced

2 tablespoons minced red onion

2 tablespoons chopped fresh cilantro leaves and tender stems

Juice of 1 lime

1 pinch sea salt

PREP AHEAD

Chop mango and pineapple

Mince jalapeño and onion

MAKE AHEAD

Refrigerate rice up to 1 week

Refrigerate salsa and salmon up to 3 days

NOTES AND SHORTCUTS

To save time, buy fresh pineapple salsa, which most grocery stores sell

Heat oven to 350°F. Lightly grease a baking sheet.

Place salmon on prepared baking sheet. Drizzle salmon with avocado oil and sprinkle with Cajun seasoning and salt. Bake for 15 to 17 minutes, until it becomes flaky in center.

To make rice: While salmon bakes, in a large skillet over medium heat, melt coconut oil. Add cauliflower rice to pan and sauté for 5 minutes. Add cilantro, coconut milk, lime juice, honey, and salt and cook for 12 to 15 minutes, until cauliflower is tender and liquid has been absorbed.

To make salsa: Meanwhile, in a small bowl, mix together mango, pineapple, jalapeño, onion, cilantro, lime juice, and salt.

Spoon salsa over salmon and serve hot with cauliflower rice.

Part 3

More Recipes

Back-Pocket Dinners

Creamy Dill-Sardine Salad with Capers

SERVES 4
ACTIVE TIME: 8 MINUTES

2 (3- to 5-ounce) tins olive oil-packed sardines

Zest and juice of 1 lemon

1 tablespoon Dijon mustard

2 tablespoons dairy-free ranch dressing

1 celery stalk, minced

1 tablespoon capers

Sea salt and black pepper

Lettuce, grain-free crackers, or toasted grain-free bread for serving

In a bowl, using a fork, mash sardines and their oil and lemon zest and juice and stir constantly until creamy. Stir in mustard, ranch dressing, celery, and capers. Season with salt and pepper.

Serve over lettuce, as a dip for crackers, or between two toasted slices of bread.

PREP AHEAD

Zest and juice lemon

Mince celery

MAKE AHEAD

Refrigerate up to 3 days

NOTES AND SHORTCUTS

Sub chopped dill pickles for capers

Sub store-bought ranch dressing, such as Tessemae's or Primal Kitchen, for homemade

Coconut-Pumpkin Curry

SERVES 4 TO 6

ACTIVE TIME: 22 MINUTES

1 tablespoon coconut oil

1 teaspoon onion powder

½ teaspoon ground ginger

2 to 3 tablespoons mild curry paste (red or yellow)

1 (15-ounce) can pumpkin puree

1 (13.5-ounce) can full-fat coconut milk

½ cup unsalted chicken bone broth or water

1½ tablespoons fish sauce

1½ teaspoons sea salt

2 cups mixed vegetables (fresh or frozen)

1 cup frozen chopped spinach

1 (13-ounce) jar soaked and sprouted chickpeas, drained

Juice of 2 limes

⅓ cup dairy-free plain yogurt (optional)

½ cup chopped dry roasted cashews (optional)

Chopped cilantro for garnish (optional)

In a large skillet over medium-high heat, melt oil. Add onion powder, ginger, and curry paste and sauté, stirring constantly, for 1 minute, until fragrant. Add pumpkin puree, coconut milk, and broth. Bring to a boil, then turn heat to medium-low and let simmer for 10 minutes, until thickened. Add fish sauce, salt, vegetables, spinach, chickpeas, and lime juice and continue to simmer for 8 to 10 minutes, until vegetables are fork-tender.

Serve hot, with a dollop of yogurt, a sprinkle of cashews, and garnished with cilantro, if desired.

NOTES AND SHORTCUTS

Sub 1 teaspoon white wine vinegar for lime juice

Sub frozen small shrimp or shredded leftover chicken for chickpeas

Use any combination of vegetables left over in fridge

Sub green onions for cilantro

Jovial brand sells soaked and pressure-cooked chickpeas that are easier on digestion

Mediterranean Salmon Salad

SERVES 4 TO 6

ACTIVE TIME: 12 MINUTES

2 (6-ounce) cans salmon

½ cup artichoke hearts, drained

½ cup pitted kalamata olives, drained

½ cup roasted red peppers, drained

¼ red onion, quartered

2 tablespoons extra-virgin olive oil

½ tablespoon red wine vinegar

½ teaspoon honey

Sea salt and cracked black pepper

½ teaspoon Healthy in a Hurry Mediterranean Seasoning (page 37)

Lettuce, grain-free pita crackers, or toasted grain-free bread for serving

Drain salmon and place in a large bowl.

In a food processor, combine artichoke hearts, olives, red peppers, and onion and pulse eight to ten times, until finely chopped. Pour mixture into bowl with salmon and mix well.

In a small bowl, whisk together oil, vinegar, honey, ½ teaspoon salt, ¼ teaspoon black pepper, and Mediterranean seasoning. Pour this dressing over salmon and stir to combine. Season with salt and pepper.

Serve over lettuce, as a dip for crackers, or between two toasted slices of bread.

PREP AHEAD

Whisk dressing

MAKE AHEAD

Refrigerate salad up to 5 days

Refrigerate dressing up to 4 weeks

NOTES AND SHORTCUTS

Sub canned tuna for salmon

Sub ½ teaspoon dried parsley, ½ teaspoon dried basil, ¼ teaspoon garlic powder, ¼ teaspoon dried oregano for Mediterranean seasoning

Tomato Soup and Grilled Prosciutto-and-Pear Cheese Sandwiches

SERVES 4
ACTIVE TIME: 35 MINUTES

SOUP

1 (28-ounce) jar marinara sauce

1 (28-ounce) can or jar fire-roasted tomatoes

2 cups unsalted chicken bone broth

1 teaspoon dried basil

¼ teaspoon garlic powder

Sea salt and cracked black pepper

¼ cup unsweetened cashew butter or coconut cream (optional)

SANDWICHES

8 slices grain-free bread or tortillas

2 tablespoons dairy-free butter

1 tablespoon Dijon mustard

2 tablespoons avocado oil mayonnaise

8 ounces crumbled dairy-free cheese (use a mix of flavors)

4 thin slices prosciutto

1 pear, thinly sliced

To make soup: In a blender, combine marinara and tomatoes. Blend on low speed until coarsely blended. Pour into a large Dutch oven and stir in broth, basil, garlic powder, 1 teaspoon salt, and ¼ teaspoon black pepper. Bring to a boil, then turn heat to medium-low and let simmer for 20 minutes. Stir in cashew butter (if using) and season with additional salt and pepper.

To prepare sandwiches: Meanwhile, set a heavy skillet or griddle over medium-low heat.

Thinly spread each slice of bread with butter and a bit of mustard. Flip and spread other sides with mayonnaise. Place two slices, mayonnaise-side down, in skillet. Divide cheese equally on top of buttered sides, and then top with a prosciutto slice and one-fourth of pear slices.

When cheese is mostly melted, using a spatula, flip one slice over on top of the other and press lightly to melt. Keep turning sandwich, pressing gently, until it is compact, both sides are crusty, and cheese is melted. Transfer to a plate. Repeat with remaining bread slices, cheese, prosciutto, and pear.

Ladle soup into individual bowls and serve with sandwiches on the side.

PREP AHEAD

Assemble sandwiches and refrigerate up to 1 day

MAKE AHEAD

Refrigerate soup up to 10 days or freeze up to 6 months

NOTES AND SHORTCUTS

Rao's is my favorite marinara sauce, for its flavor and clean ingredients

Sub vegetable broth to be vegan

Miyoko's brand butter, Miyoko's mozzarella, and Violife feta are a winning combination here

For dairy cheese, try a combination of sheep's milk Manchego and Lamb Chopper by Cypress Grove

Tuna Casserole

SERVES 4 TO 6
ACTIVE TIME: 40 MINUTES

Sea salt

2 (8-ounce) boxes
grain-free fusilli

3 cups Cream of Mushroom
Soup (page 173)

⅔ cup dairy-free milk

3 (5-ounce) cans water-packed
tuna, drained

1 cup frozen peas

1 celery stalk, finely chopped

2 cups shredded cheese
(optional)

Cracked black pepper

1 (5.5-ounce) bag avocado-oil
potato chips, crushed

Green salad for serving

Preheat oven to 425°F.

Fill a large pot with water and bring to a boil. Add a pinch of salt, stir in fusilli, and cook for 8 to 10 minutes, until tender but still firm. Drain.

In a large bowl, mix together fusilli, soup, milk, tuna, peas, celery, and 1 cup cheese (if using). Season with salt and pepper.

Transfer mixture to a 9 by 13-inch baking dish and top with potato chips and remaining 1 cup cheese. Bake for 18 to 20 minutes, until edges are bubbling.

Serve hot with a green salad.

PREP AHEAD

Cook and drain pasta

Defrost mushroom soup, if frozen

Chop celery

Crush potato chips

MAKE AHEAD

Refrigerate mushroom soup up to 7 days or freeze up to 6 months

Assemble casserole, minus chips, and refrigerate up to 3 days or freeze up to 3 months; add chips just before baking

NOTES AND SHORTCUTS

Sub cooked zucchini noodles or spaghetti squash for pasta

Crumble Miyoko's mozzarella or Violife feta for dairy-free

For dairy cheese, try a combination of sheep's milk Manchego and Lamb Chopper by Cypress Grove or a sharp Cheddar

Sub plantain chips or ground crispy pork rinds for potato chips

Sub unsalted chicken bone broth for dairy-free milk

Sub canned chicken for tuna

Unfortunately, there aren't any brands that offer dairy-free mushroom soup, so this must be made in advance. If dairy is tolerated, purchase a gluten-free brand such as Pacific Foods.

Breakfast-for-Dinner: Sheet-Pan Pancakes and Bacon

SERVES 4 TO 6

ACTIVE TIME: 28 MINUTES

2 (12-ounce/340g) packs sugar- and nitrate-free bacon

3 eggs

¾ cup (175ml) unsweetened almond milk

2 cups (295g) grain-free vanilla cake mix

1 tablespoon melted ghee or avocado oil

Mix-ins: Blueberries; sliced peaches, bananas, or strawberries; chocolate chips; or chopped walnuts (optional)

Maple syrup, fruit jams, ghee or butter, and whipped coconut cream for serving

Line two baking sheets with parchment paper. Line a plate with paper towels.

Place bacon in a single layer on a prepared baking sheet. Place in oven, set temperature to 400°F, and bake for 12 minutes.

Meanwhile, in a blender, combine eggs, almond milk, cake mix, and ghee and blend on high speed for 30 seconds, until a smooth batter forms.

Spread batter onto second prepared baking sheet. Line batter with desired mix-ins.

Remove bacon from oven and flip pieces over. Place bacon pan on top rack and batter pan on center rack. Bake for 10 to 12 minutes more, then transfer bacon to prepared plate to drain.

Cut pancakes into squares and serve with maple syrup, jams, ghee, and whipped coconut cream, along with bacon.

MAKE AHEAD

Refrigerate bacon and pancakes up to 7 days

Let pancakes cool, then freeze individual squares up to 6 months; reheat in toaster

NOTES AND SHORTCUTS

The fun part about this recipe is letting kids pick individual toppings, then dividing batter into quarters so they get to sprinkle on what they want! Plus, there's no time spent over a griddle flipping individual cakes, and bacon cooks at same time.

Any grain-free cake mix or pancake mix will work here, but I prefer Simple Mills. Be sure to use one that has sweetener and leavener (baking soda or baking powder), since it is not included in this recipe.

Scan QR code to sub a homemade flour mix (with a nut-free option) for store-bought

Tuna Salad with Apples and Pumpkin Seeds

SERVES 4
ACTIVE TIME: 12 MINUTES

3 (5-ounce) cans water-packed tuna, drained

¾ cup avocado oil mayonnaise

2 tablespoons minced red onion

2 tablespoons minced dill pickles

½ teaspoon dried dill

1 teaspoon yellow mustard

Sea salt and cracked black pepper

1 tart apple, chopped

¼ cup sprouted, salted pumpkin seeds

Lettuce, grain-free crackers, or toasted grain-free bread for serving

Place tuna in a small bowl. Using a fork, break apart and mix in mayonnaise, onion, pickles, dill, mustard, ½ teaspoon salt, and ¼ teaspoon black pepper. Gently fold in apples and pumpkin seeds.

Serve in lettuce cups, as a dip for crackers, or between slices of bread.

PREP AHEAD

Mince onion

Mince pickles

MAKE AHEAD

Refrigerate up to 5 days

NOTES AND SHORTCUTS

Sub canned salmon for tuna

Lemony Shrimp Pasta with Artichokes

SERVES 4 TO 6

ACTIVE TIME: 30 MINUTES

¾ pound frozen shrimp, peeled and deveined

8 cups water

Olive oil for drizzling

16 ounces dried grain-free pasta

3 tablespoons ghee

6 garlic cloves, pressed or grated

Zest and juice of 1 lemon

1 (14-ounce) can artichoke hearts, drained and chopped

¾ teaspoon sea salt

¼ teaspoon cracked black pepper

¼ teaspoon red pepper flakes

Fresh herbs, such as parsley, dill, basil, or chives for serving (optional)

Place shrimp in a colander and set inside a bowl of lukewarm water.

In a stockpot, bring salted water to a boil. Add a drizzle of oil and the pasta and cook, stirring frequently, for about 11 minutes, until pasta is al dente.

Meanwhile, in a large skillet over medium heat, melt ghee. Add garlic and sauté for 5 minutes, until golden brown. Drain shrimp and pat dry. Add to skillet and sauté for 2 to 4 minutes, until nearly cooked through. Using a slotted spoon, remove shrimp and set aside on a plate.

Drain pasta and reserve ¾ cup cooking water. Add reserved pasta water to skillet, turn heat to high, and bring to a boil. Then turn heat to medium-low and let simmer until sauce has reduced by about half. Remove from heat and stir in lemon zest and juice and artichoke hearts. Return shrimp to pan with drained pasta and toss to coat. Sprinkle with salt, black pepper, red pepper flakes, and herbs (if using).

Serve hot.

PREP AHEAD

Defrost shrimp

Press or grate garlic

Zest and juice lemon

Drain and chop artichokes

MAKE AHEAD

Refrigerate pasta, minus shrimp, up to 1 week; add shrimp just before serving

---

NOTES AND SHORTCUTS

Sub extra-virgin olive oil for ghee

Grain-free pasta, such as cassava or chickpea, typically comes in boxes that are 8 ounces, while gluten-free pasta, such as brown rice, lentil, or quinoa, typically comes in boxes that are 12 ounces. Use 2 boxes of grain-free pasta or 1¼ boxes of gluten-free.

Sub zucchini noodles for pasta; pan-fry in a dry skillet until tender, then add to sauce

Water should be starchy in order to create a sauce, so be sure to use only 8 cups water to boil pasta

Sub canned chickpeas for shrimp

SAUSAGE SKILLETS, FOUR WAYS

SERVES 4 TO 6
ACTIVE TIME: 25 TO 30 MINUTES

Brats and Sauerkraut

1½ pounds baby red potatoes, halved

3 tablespoons avocado oil

1 bunch curly kale, ribs removed and chopped

1 small yellow onion, thinly sliced

4 garlic cloves, crushed with a garlic press

Zest and juice of 1 lemon

1 (12-ounce) package cooked bratwurst sausage links, sliced 1 inch thick

1 teaspoon sea salt

¼ teaspoon cracked black pepper

⅓ cup sauerkraut, drained

2 tablespoons grainy mustard

Bring large pot of salted water to boil. Add halved potatoes and cook for 5 to 7 minutes, until fork-tender. Drain.

In large skillet over medium-high heat, warm 2 tablespoons of oil until it shimmers. Add boiled potatoes, cut-side down, and cook without stirring for 6 to 8 minutes, until well browned on bottoms. Stir and continue cooking for 1 to 2 minutes, until browned all over. Remove to a plate.

Add remaining 1 tablespoon oil to skillet. Add kale, onion, garlic, and lemon zest and juice and sauté for 5 to 7 minutes, until kale wilts and onions soften. Add bratwurst and cook for 2 to 3 minutes, until heated through and slightly browned. Return browned potatoes to skillet and remove from heat. Stir in salt, black pepper, and sauerkraut. Dollop grainy mustard over top and serve hot.

PREP AHEAD

Halve and parboil red potatoes and refrigerate up to 1 week

Remove ribs and chop kale

Slice onions

Peel and crush garlic

Slice sausages

Autumn Chicken Apple

3 tablespoons avocado oil

1 (16-ounce) package frozen butternut squash cubes

1 (5-ounce) package baby spinach

1 small yellow onion, thinly sliced

1 tart apple, diced

1 (12-ounce) package cooked chicken-apple sausage links, sliced 1 inch thick

1 teaspoon Healthy in a Hurry Burnt Broccoli Seasoning (page 36)

3 tablespoons honey-mustard dressing

PREP AHEAD

Slice onion

Dice apple

Slice sausages

In a large skillet over medium-high heat, warm 2 tablespoons oil until it shimmers. Add butternut squash and cook 6 to 8 minutes, stirring occasionally, until well browned. Remove to a plate.

Add remaining 1 tablespoon oil to the skillet. Add spinach, onion, and apple and sauté for 5 to 7 minutes, until spinach wilts and onions soften. Add sausage and cook for 2 to 3 minutes, until heated through and slightly browned. Return butternut squash to skillet. Stir in seasoning and drizzle with honey-mustard dressing. Serve hot.

Spicy Cajun

PREP AHEAD

Dice and parboil sweet potatoes and refrigerate up to 1 week

Remove ribs and chop collards

Slice onion

Dice bell peppers and zucchini

Slice sausages

1 pound sweet potatoes, scrubbed clean and diced

3 tablespoons avocado oil

1 bunch collard greens, ribs removed and chopped

1 small yellow onion, thinly sliced

2 red bell peppers, seeded and diced

2 zucchini, diced

1 (12-ounce) package cooked andouille sausage links, sliced 1 inch thick

1 teaspoon Healthy in a Hurry Cajun Seasoning (page 37)

3 tablespoons chipotle mayonnaise

Bring a large pot of salted water to a boil. Add sweet potatoes and cook for 5 to 7 minutes, until fork-tender. Drain.

In a large skillet over medium-high heat, warm 2 tablespoons of oil until it shimmers. Add cooked sweet potatoes, cut-side down, and cook without stirring for 6 to 8 minutes, until well browned on bottoms. Stir and continue cooking for 1 to 2 minutes, until browned all over. Remove to a plate.

Add remaining 1 tablespoon of oil to skillet. Add collard greens, onion, bell peppers, and zucchini and sauté for 5 to 7 minutes, until greens wilt and vegetables soften. Add sausage and cook for 2 to 3 minutes, until heated through and slightly browned. Return sweet potatoes to skillet and remove from heat. Stir in seasoning and dollop chipotle mayonnaise over top.

Serve hot.

Roasted Tomato Italian

1½ pounds parsnips, diced

3 tablespoons avocado oil

1 bunch lacinato kale, ribs removed and chopped

1 small yellow onion, thinly sliced

1 pint cherry tomatoes, halved

1 (12-ounce) package cooked sweet Italian sausage links, sliced 1 inch thick

¾ teaspoon Healthy in a Hurry Mediterranean Seasoning (page 37)

3 tablespoons dairy-free pesto

Bring a large pot of salted water to a boil. Add parsnips and cook for 5 to 7 minutes, until fork-tender. Drain.

In a large skillet over medium-high heat, warm 2 tablespoons of oil until it shimmers. Add cooked parsnips, cut-side down, and cook without stirring for 6 to 8 minutes, until well browned. Stir and continue cooking for 1 to 2 minutes, until browned all over. Remove to a plate.

Add the remaining 1 tablespoon of oil to the skillet. Add kale, onion, and cherry tomatoes and sauté for 5 to 7 minutes, until kale wilts and onion softens. Add sausage to the skillet and cook for 2 to 3 minutes, until heated through and slightly browned. Return parsnips to skillet and remove from heat. Stir in seasoning and dollop pesto over top. Serve hot.

PREP AHEAD

Dice and parboil parsnips and refrigerate up to 1 week

Remove ribs and chop kale

Slice onion

Halve tomatoes

Slice sausages

MAKE AHEAD

Refrigerate up to 1 week

Freeze up to 4 months

NOTES AND SHORTCUTS

Just like meatballs, cooked sausages are great to keep on hand in fridge or freezer for an easy skillet dinner. They last for weeks, refrigerated, or months, frozen, and are easy to defrost. Choose between chicken, pork, or beef; look for brands with no added sugars or nitrates, such as Whole Foods brand, Aidells, Bilinski's, Niman Ranch, and Teton Waters Ranch.

Sub grain-free gnocchi, such as Trader Joe's or Cappello's, for potatoes

Sub peeled and diced celeriac or parsnips for potatoes

My Healthy in a Hurry seasoning blends (see page 27) are quick flavor boosters here, but simply using salt and pepper to taste will also work

Spiced Sweet Potato Soup

SERVES 4
ACTIVE TIME: 15 MINUTES

1 (13.5-ounce) can full-fat coconut milk

1 tablespoon avocado oil

2 tablespoons mild curry paste (red or yellow)

1 tablespoon curry powder

Cracked black pepper

2 cups unsalted vegetable broth

1 (15-ounce) can sweet potato puree

1 (18-ounce) jar diced tomatoes

1 (13-ounce) jar soaked and sprouted chickpeas, drained

2 tablespoons pure maple syrup

Sea salt

1 teaspoon white wine vinegar

¼ cup chopped dry roasted cashews

½ cup chopped fresh herbs, such as cilantro, mint, scallions, or chives

Spoon 2 tablespoons of thick cream from top of coconut milk and set aside.

In a large stockpot over medium-high heat, warm oil until it shimmers. Add curry paste, curry powder, and ½ teaspoon black pepper and sauté for about 15 seconds, until fragrant. Stir in coconut milk, broth, sweet potato puree, tomatoes, chickpeas, maple syrup, and 2 teaspoons salt. Bring to a boil, then turn heat to medium-low and let simmer for 10 minutes. Using an immersion blender, blend soup until chickpeas are coarsely chopped but some texture remains. Season with salt and pepper and stir in vinegar.

Serve hot with a dollop of coconut cream, cashews, and a generous pinch of fresh herbs.

MAKE AHEAD

Refrigerate up to 10 days or freeze up to 6 months

NOTES AND SHORTCUTS

Sub pumpkin puree for sweet potato puree

Sub honey for maple syrup

Sub toasted pepitas for cashews

Sub 2 cups pine nuts for chickpeas

Jovial brand sells soaked and pressure-cooked chickpeas that are easier on digestion

Mekhala and Thai Kitchen make paleo-friendly curry paste

Add shrimp or shredded rotisserie chicken

Baked Pesto Gnocchi and Sausage

SERVES 4
ACTIVE TIME: 28 MINUTES

2 (10- to 12-ounce) packages grain-free gnocchi

1 (12-ounce) package cooked chicken Italian sausage links (sweet or spicy)

1 (16-ounce) package frozen butternut squash cubes

3 tablespoons avocado oil

1 teaspoon Healthy in a Hurry Mediterranean Seasoning (page 37)

½ teaspoon sea salt

1 ounce dried mixed mushrooms, rehydrated in hot water

6 ounces dairy-free pesto (optional)

Arrange two racks to divide oven into thirds. Preheat oven to 450°F.

On a baking sheet, combine, gnocchi, sausages, and squash, then drizzle with oil and sprinkle with Mediterranean seasoning and salt. Toss to coat and spread in an even layer. Place baking sheet on lower rack.

Bake for 18 to 20 minutes, stirring halfway through, until squash is fork-tender. Stir in mushrooms, move baking sheet to upper rack, and turn oven to broil. Broil until gnocchi are browned and crisp on edges, 3 to 5 minutes.

Slice sausages and serve drizzled with pesto, if desired.

PREP AHEAD

Rehydrate mushrooms

MAKE AHEAD

Refrigerate up to 1 week

Freeze up to 4 months

NOTES AND SHORTCUTS

This recipe is intentionally simple and versatile, so it can be added to your rotation as a backup or "night off" from cooking. There's no chopping required, and different seasonings and sauces are interchangeable with what you have on hand.

Sub chicken apple sausage or andouille for Italian sausage

Sub any of your favorite seasoning blends for Mediterranean Seasoning

Sausage brands: Bilinski's, Aidells, and Pederson's Natural Farms

Sub Green Goddess Dressing (page 33) for pesto

Cappello's and Trader Joe's offer grain-free and gluten-free gnocchi

Sub blanched diced sweet potatoes for gnocchi

Sub frozen mushrooms for dried

Sub marinara sauce for pesto

Tequila-lime chicken with Coconut-Lime Cauli Rice (page 269) or Roasted Pineapple and Sweet Potatoes with Cinnamon-Cashew Drizzle (page 272)

Moroccan chicken with Coconut-Lime Cauli Rice (page 269) or Curried Vegetables (page 271)

BBQ chicken with Mashed Roots (page 142) or Instant Pot Mashed Potatoes (page 273)

Greek chicken with Mediterranean Roasted Vegetables (page 118) or Broccoli-Crunch Salad (page 268)

FOUR QUICK-GRILLED CHICKEN MARINADES

SERVES 4 TO 6 PER MARINADE
ACTIVE TIME: 6 HOURS

3 pounds boneless, skinless chicken breasts or thighs

Place chicken in a large resealable bag. Add chosen marinade ingredients, seal bag, and toss to coat. Refrigerate for at least 6 and up to 48 hours.

When ready to cook, prepare a grill for medium heat, then grill until temperature registers 165°F on an instant-read thermometer. Serve hot with suggested sides (see page 246).

Tequila-Lime Marinade

2 tablespoons avocado oil

2 tablespoons tequila

Juice of 1 lime

¼ cup Healthy in a Hurry Taco Seasoning (page 37)

Moroccan Marinade

1 cup unsweetened dairy-free yogurt

Zest of 1 lemon, plus 2 teaspoons lemon juice

3 tablespoons Heathy in a Hurry Tagine Seasoning (page 37)

1 teaspoon sea salt

BBQ Marinade

2 tablespoons Healthy in a Hurry BBQ Rub (page 36)

1 cup unsweetened ketchup

2 tablespoons date syrup

1 teaspoon sea salt

Greek Marinade

3 tablespoons extra-virgin olive oil

Juice of 1 lemon

2 tablespoons Healthy in a Hurry Mediterranean Seasoning (page 37)

MAKE AHEAD

Refrigerate up to 2 days

Freeze up to 3 months. Defrost for 24 hours in refrigerator before cooking. For a quick defrost, submerge bag in a bowl of room-temperature water for 1 hour.

NOTES AND SHORTCUTS

Purchase chicken in bulk to save

Combine these marinades with eyeball measurements to save time

These are recipes I call my fallback recipes. When life gets busy and I need something without a lot of thought, I pull one of these out and serve the grilled chicken alongside a salad, grilled vegetables, or one of the sides listed opposite.

Make-Ahead Breakfasts

Blueberry Muffins

MAKES 12 MUFFINS
ACTIVE TIME: 28 MINUTES

3 eggs

⅓ cup (80ml) unsweetened almond milk

¼ cup (60ml) melted ghee

¼ cup (85g) light-colored raw honey

¼ cup (40g) maple sugar

1 teaspoon vanilla extract

2 cups (295g) grain-free vanilla cake mix

Zest and juice of 1 small lemon

1 cup (140g) fresh blueberries or frozen wild blueberries, thawed and drained

Preheat oven to 350°F. Line a 12-cup muffin pan with parchment paper liners.

In a blender, combine eggs, almond milk, ghee, honey, maple sugar, and vanilla and blend on high speed for 15 seconds. Add cake mix and blend again for 30 to 45 seconds on high speed, until well combined and creamy. Add lemon zest and juice and ¾ cup (105g) blueberries and stir gently with a wooden spoon. Fill muffin cups nearly to top. Place remaining ¼ cup (35g) blueberries on tops of each.

Bake for 20 to 25 minutes, until a toothpick comes out clean when inserted into center of a muffin. Allow to cool for 10 minutes in pan, then transfer muffins to a wire rack to cool completely before serving.

———————

PREP AHEAD

Zest and juice lemon

Wash or defrost and drain blueberries

———————

MAKE AHEAD

Refrigerate up to 10 days

Freeze up to 6 months

TIPS AND SHORTCUTS

Any grain-free cake mix or even pancake mix will work here, but I prefer making my own to save money and control ingredients. Simple Mills or Bob's Red Mill grain-free cake mixes work best for store-bought; be sure to use one that has sweetener and leavener (baking soda or baking powder), since it is not included in these recipes.

Scan QR code to sub a homemade flour mix (with a nut-free option) for store-bought cake mix

Sub avocado oil for ghee

Sub cranberries for blueberries

Savory Sausage–Chive Breakfast Muffins

SERVES 14
ACTIVE TIME: 25 MINUTES

8 eggs

1 cup (240ml) unsweetened dairy-free milk

½ cup (120ml) extra-virgin olive oil

1 cup (120g) arrowroot powder

1 cup (110g) chickpea flour

½ cup (60g) coconut flour

½ cup (85g) hulled hemp hearts, plus more for topping

2 tablespoons nutritional yeast (optional)

1 tablespoon grain-free baking powder

2 teaspoons apple cider vinegar

2 teaspoons sea salt

½ teaspoon cracked black pepper

2 bunches chives, chopped

2 cups (160g) chopped Swiss chard

7- or 8-ounce box frozen breakfast sausage links, chopped

Preheat oven to 350°F. Line a 12-cup muffin pan with parchment paper liners.

In a blender, combine eggs, milk, oil, arrowroot powder, chickpea flour, coconut flour, hemp hearts, nutritional yeast (if using), baking powder, vinegar, salt, and pepper and blend on high speed until a smooth batter forms.

Reserve 1 tablespoon chopped chives. Stir remaining chives, chard, and sausage into batter. Carefully pour batter into prepared muffin cups, filling two-thirds full. Sprinkle reserved chives over tops of muffins and top each with some hemp hearts.

Bake for 18 to 20 minutes, until a toothpick comes out clean when inserted into center of a muffin. Let cool on a wire rack for 10 minutes and then serve warm.

_____

PREP AHEAD

Chop chives

Chop chard

Chop sausage

_____

MAKE AHEAD

Refrigerate up to 5 days

Freeze up to 6 months

NOTES AND SHORTCUTS

Chickpea flour or garbanzo bean flour adds protein and great structure to these muffins. I use sprouted chickpea flour for easier digestion. Thrive Market, PureLiving, or To Your Health all sell it.

Sub 1¼ cups (125g) almond flour or ½ cup (60g) cassava flour for chickpea flour

Sub green onions for chives

Sub chopped, cooked bacon for sausage

Sub 1 cup shredded sheep's milk cheese, such as Manchego or Pecorino Romano, or crumbled goat cheese for nutritional yeast

Sub frozen spinach, thawed and pressed to remove excess liquid, for chard

Make vegetarian by subbing ½ cup chopped sun-dried tomatoes for sausage

Make-Ahead Poached Eggs

SERVES 4 TO 6

ACTIVE TIME: 15 MINUTES

1 teaspoon sea salt

2 teaspoons white vinegar

6 to 12 eggs, cold

Fill a bowl with ice-cold water.

In a large skillet over medium heat, add enough water to reach 1 inch up side, then add salt and vinegar and bring to a simmer.

Crack each egg separately into a custard cup or small ramekin.

Using a spoon, stir water in one direction to create a gentle vortex. Carefully drop eggs, one at a time, into center of whirlpool.

Turn off heat, cover pan, and set a timer for 5 minutes. Using a slotted spoon, transfer eggs to ice bath.

Refrigerate eggs in the ice bath for up to 5 days. To reheat, warm in hot water for 2 to 3 minutes.

NOTES AND SHORTCUTS

I like the whirlpool method of poaching eggs because it keeps the egg whites together, but there are many ways to poach eggs, so use the method you are most comfortable with.

Instant Pot Soft-Boiled Eggs

SERVES 4 TO 6

ACTIVE TIME: 12 MINUTES

6 to 12 eggs

Add 1½ cups water to an Instant Pot. Place as many eggs as you can in a single layer to fill bottom of a steamer basket or on machine's wire rack. (Depending on size of machine, you may need to do this in two batches.)

Secure lid and set valve to seal. Cook on high pressure with a 3-minute timer. Quick-release pressure so eggs stop cooking.

Place hot eggs into cool water to halt cooking and to let cool enough to handle. Peel and enjoy.

MAKE AHEAD

Refrigerate up to 7 days

NOTES AND SHORTCUTS

Hard- or soft-boiling eggs in an Instant Pot makes shells practically fall off when peeling.

Increase time to 5 minutes for yolks that are cooked almost completely through but still soft. Increase time to 7 minutes for fully cooked yolks. You may need to play with time, depending on size and freshness of eggs.

Golden Chia Parfaits with Tropical Fruit

SERVES 6

ACTIVE TIME: 10 MINUTES

2 cups frozen mango pieces, thawed

1 (13.5-ounce) can full-fat coconut milk

1 cup plain dairy-free yogurt

2 tablespoons pure maple syrup

1 teaspoon ground turmeric

1 teaspoon vanilla extract

1 pinch sea salt

½ cup white chia seeds

Dragon fruit, kiwi, lychee, papaya, pineapple, or passion fruit and toasted unsweetened coconut for topping

In a large bowl, using a fork, mash mango, then whisk in coconut milk, yogurt, maple syrup, turmeric, vanilla, and salt. Pour in chia seeds and stir to mix well. Divide mixture among six small jars or bowls and refrigerate overnight.

Top with diced fruit and toasted coconut before serving.

PREP AHEAD

Peel and dice fruit

MAKE AHEAD

Refrigerate up to 1 week

Freeze up to 4 months

NOTES AND SHORTCUTS

Sub frozen fruit for fresh

Cocojune and Culina are my favorite brands for dairy-free plain yogurt

Sub organic Greek-style dairy-free yogurt for higher protein

Bacon and Hash Brown Tray Bake

SERVES 4 TO 6

ACTIVE TIME: 35 MINUTES

10 slices sugar- and nitrate-free bacon

2 (12-ounce) packages frozen shredded hash browns

2 teaspoons Healthy in a Hurry Fries Seasoning Salt (page 36)

8 eggs

Sea salt and cracked black pepper

1 small bunch chives, chopped

Line a half sheet pan with parchment paper. Line a plate with paper towels.

Place bacon in a single layer on prepared sheet pan. Turn oven temperature to 425°F and place pan on center rack.

Bake for 10 to 12 minutes, until bacon is mostly cooked but still soft. Remove bacon from pan and place on prepared plate to drain. Pour off all but 2 tablespoons bacon grease from pan.

Add hash browns to bacon grease. Sprinkle with fry seasoning and toss to coat.

Place sheet pan back in oven on top rack and bake potatoes until edges begin to brown, 15 to 17 minutes.

Once bacon has cooled, coarsely chop.

Remove sheet pan from oven and toss potatoes. Smooth potatoes into a single layer, then create eight wells in hash browns. Gently crack eggs into wells, keeping yolks intact. Sprinkle eggs with salt and pepper and add chopped bacon.

Return sheet pan to top rack and bake until egg whites have set but yolks are still runny and potatoes have crisped on top, 2 to 4 minutes longer.

Garnish with chives and serve immediately.

MAKE AHEAD

Refrigerate up to 5 days; reheat in a 300°F oven for 10 to 15 minutes

NOTES AND SHORTCUTS

Cascadian Farm sells an organic blend of shredded frozen potatoes, carrots, and sweet potatoes that works wonderfully here, as will 1 pound peeled potatoes or sweet potatoes, grated with a food processor or box grater

Sub Everything Bagel seasoning or your favorite meat and potatoes seasoning for fries seasoning salt

Bacon-Spinach Sandwiches

SERVES 8
ACTIVE TIME: 32 MINUTES

1 (8-ounce) package sugar- and nitrate-free bacon

12 eggs

2 cups fresh baby spinach, coarsely chopped

⅓ cup unsweetened dairy-free milk

1½ teaspoons sea salt

¼ teaspoon cracked pepper

16 cauliflower sandwich thins

3 tablespoons avocado oil mayonnaise

Line a baking sheet with parchment paper. Grease an 8 by 8-inch baking dish.

Lay bacon on prepared sheet pan and place in oven on top rack. Preheat the oven to 325°F.

In prepared baking dish, combine eggs, spinach, milk, salt, and black pepper and whisk together. Bake for 18 to 20 minutes, until just set and pulling away from dish slightly. Remove from oven and let cool. Continue cooking bacon until it has reached desired doneness, 5 to 7 minutes longer.

Cut eggs into eight squares, a similar size as your sandwich thins, or use a biscuit cutter to cut circles.

Put an egg square on bottom of each of eight thins. Top with bacon. Swipe mayonnaise onto remaining eight top thins and place on top of sandwiches. Let sandwiches cool, until no longer steaming, then wrap tightly in parchment paper. Store in a resealable bag or container.

VARIATIONS:

Ham and Cheese Sandwiches

Omit bacon and spinach and add 8 slices sugar-free deli ham and 8 slices grass-fed or dairy-free Cheddar cheese to the sandwiches when assembling.

Feta, Sun-Dried Tomato, and Pesto Sandwiches

Omit bacon and mayonnaise. Add 1/3 cup dairy-free feta cheese and 1/3 cup sun-dried tomatoes to egg mixture before baking. Swipe pesto onto rounds in lieu of mayonnaise.

PREP AHEAD

Crack and whisk eggs

MAKE AHEAD

Refrigerate up to 5 days

Freeze up to 6 months

Reheat defrosted sandwiches, still in parchment, in a 425°F oven for 15 minutes. From frozen, 25 to 30 minutes. If available, convection settings help to crisp cauliflower rounds. Microwave for 2 to 3 minutes on high from frozen.

NOTES AND SHORTCUTS

A high-fat-content milk, such as full-fat coconut milk or cashew milk, works best

Outer Aisle and Trader Joe's both carry cauliflower sandwich thins; they do contain dairy, but are low to lactose-free

For dairy-free, substitute gluten-free English muffins, grain-free bread, hamburger buns, or homemade grain-free bagels for cauliflower thins

Sub chard or kale for spinach

To add cheese: Gruyère, sheep's milk Manchego, or dairy-free Violife feta all lend well to freeze-and-reheat method

Label the sandwiches after wrapping in parchment if you make different flavors

Make-Ahead Snacks

Coconut-Chocolate Hunks

SERVES 16
ACTIVE TIME: 10 MINUTES

⅓ cup coconut oil

¼ cup honey

1½ cups unsweetened shredded coconut

¼ cup arrowroot powder

2 tablespoons coconut flour

¼ cup coconut sugar

3 tablespoons ground golden flaxseed

2 tablespoons unsweetened almond butter

¼ teaspoon sea salt

½ cup chocolate chips

Line a loaf pan with parchment paper.

In a small saucepan over low heat, melt coconut oil and honey. Set aside to cool.

In a food processor, combine shredded coconut, arrowroot, coconut flour, coconut sugar, flaxseed, almond butter, and salt and pulse three to five times to incorporate. Pour in coconut oil–honey mixture and use a wooden spoon to blend well. Let cool to room temperature, then stir in chocolate chips.

Press dough into prepared pan and freeze until set, about 1 hour. Remove parchment and cut into bite-size squares to serve.

MAKE AHEAD

Store at room temperature up to 1 week

Refrigerate up to 1 month

Freeze up to 6 months

NOTES AND SHORTCUTS

Mixture can be rolled into energy balls

Sub sunflower seed butter for almond butter

Sub dried fruit for chocolate chips

Use expeller-pressed coconut oil to minimize coconut taste

French Onion Dip

SERVES 6 TO 8

ACTIVE TIME: 30 MINUTES

2 tablespoons avocado oil

1½ cups diced yellow onions

Sea salt

1½ cups dairy-free sour cream
or plain yogurt

¼ cup avocado oil mayonnaise

⅓ cup dairy-free cream cheese

1 teaspoon onion powder

½ teaspoon garlic powder

Ground white pepper

Fresh-cut vegetables,
avocado-oil potato chips, or
plantain chips for serving

In a skillet over medium-low heat, warm oil until it shimmers.
Add onions and ½ teaspoon salt, then turn heat to low and
caramelize onions for 20 to 25 minutes, stirring occasionally.
Set aside to cool.

In a small bowl, mix together sour cream, mayonnaise,
cream cheese, onion powder, garlic powder, and ¼ teaspoon
white pepper. Stir in caramelized onions and season with salt
and pepper. Cover and refrigerate overnight.

Serve with vegetables or chips.

PREP AHEAD

Dice onion

MAKE AHEAD

Refrigerate up to 10 days

Freeze up to 4 months

NOTES AND SHORTCUTS

Dairy-free sour cream and yogurt
brands: Forager, Cocojune, and Culina

Dairy-free cream cheese brands:
Miyoko's and Violife

Sub organic lactose-free sour cream
and cream cheese such as Green
Valley or Good Culture

Smoked Salmon Dip

SERVES 6 TO 8
ACTIVE TIME: 30 MINUTES

8 ounces dairy-free cream cheese

½ cup dairy-free plain yogurt

2 dill sprigs, chopped

2 tablespoons capers, drained and chopped

1 teaspoon prepared horseradish

1 squeeze fresh lemon juice

½ teaspoon sea salt

¼ teaspoon cracked black pepper

¼ teaspoon hot sauce

4 ounces smoked salmon, chopped

Fresh-cut vegetables, avocado-oil potato chips, plantain chips, or grain-free pita crackers for serving

In a medium bowl, mix together cream cheese, yogurt, dill, capers, horseradish, lemon juice, sea salt, black pepper, and hot sauce. Gently fold in salmon. Cover and refrigerate overnight.

Serve with vegetables, chips, or crackers.

PREP AHEAD

Chop dill

Chop capers

Chop salmon

———————

MAKE AHEAD

Refrigerate up to 10 days

Freeze up to 4 months

———————

NOTES AND SHORTCUTS

Dairy-free yogurt brands: Forager, Cocojune, and Culina

Dairy-free cream cheese brands: Miyoko's and Violife

Sub organic lactose-free sour cream and cream cheese, such as Green Valley or Good Culture

Sub spicy mustard for prepared horseradish

Sub chives for dill

Ranch Snack Mix

SERVES 10

ACTIVE TIME: 1 HOUR, 35 MINUTES

¼ cup melted ghee

1½ tablespoons coconut aminos

¼ teaspoon fresh lime juice

2 teaspoons garlic powder

1 teaspoon onion powder

1 teaspoon sea salt

1 teaspoon dried parsley

¾ teaspoon dried dill

¾ teaspoon dried chives

¼ teaspoon cracked black pepper

5 ounces plantain chips

1 cup grain-free pretzels

1 cup grain-free crackers

1 cup whole raw cashews

½ cup raw sunflower seeds

Preheat oven to 200°F.

In a large bowl, mix together ghee, coconut aminos, lime juice, garlic powder, onion powder, salt, parsley, dill, chives, and black pepper.

Pour chips, pretzels, crackers, cashews, and sunflower seeds on a baking sheet and drizzle ghee mixture over top, using your hands to coat. Gently distribute into a single layer.

Bake for 90 minutes, stirring every 20 to 30 minutes. Remove from oven and let cool completely on a wire rack. Transfer to an airtight container.

PREP AHEAD

Combine ghee mixture

MAKE AHEAD

Store at room temperature up to 1 month

NOTES AND SHORTCUTS

Sub avocado oil for ghee

Simple Mills and FitJoy are my favorite snack brands

Cherry-Walnut Protein Cookies

SERVES 12
ACTIVE TIME: 22 MINUTES

½ cup (120g) almond butter

¼ cup (30g) coconut flour

6 pitted dried dates, soaked in warm water for 15 minutes

¾ cups (60g) shredded unsweetened coconut

½ cup (120ml) unsweetened applesauce

2 eggs

2 teaspoons ground cinnamon

1 teaspoon vanilla extract

½ teaspoon baking soda

¼ teaspoon sea salt

3 tablespoons currants

2 tablespoons dried dark cherries, fruit-juice sweetened

2 tablespoons chopped walnuts

Preheat oven to 350°F. Line a baking sheet with parchment paper or a silicone mat.

In a food processor, combine almond butter, coconut flour, and dates and process for 1 minute, until well combined and dates have broken into really small pieces. Add coconut, applesauce, eggs, cinnamon, vanilla, baking soda, and salt and process for 30 seconds, until a wet dough forms. Add currants, cherries, and walnuts and pulse once or twice, until fruit is coarsely chopped and incorporated.

Using a cookie scoop or two large spoons, drop dough in heaping spoonfuls onto prepared baking sheet. Dip a metal spatula in water and use bottom to lightly press each dough ball. Since cookies will not spread or rise, make sure to shape prior to baking.

Bake for 12 to 15 minutes, until golden on top and slightly brown along edges. Let cool before serving.

MAKE AHEAD

Store at room temperature up to 1 week

Refrigerate up to 2 weeks

Freeze up to 6 months

NOTES AND SHORTCUTS

Sub 2 tablespoons finely ground flaxseed plus 5 tablespoons (74ml) warm water for eggs; whisk and let sit for 5 to 10 minutes, until thickened

Sub fruit-juice sweetened dried cranberries for cherries

Sub raisins for currants

Sub chocolate chips for dried fruit

Buffalo Bacon Deviled Eggs

SERVES 12
ACTIVE TIME: 25 MINUTES

12 eggs

¼ cup avocado oil mayonnaise

¼ cup full-fat coconut milk

2 teaspoons Dijon mustard

2 tablespoons buffalo wing sauce

½ teaspoon onion powder

¼ teaspoon sea salt

2 slices cooked sugar- and nitrate-free bacon, chopped

1 green onion, white and tender green parts, chopped

Add 1½ cups water to a 6-quart Instant Pot. Place as many eggs as you can in a single layer to fill bottom of a steamer basket or on machine's wire rack. Stack another basket gently on top and add remaining eggs. Secure lid and set valve to seal. Cook at high pressure with a 5-minute timer. Quick-release pressure. Place hot eggs into cool water to halt cooking process and become cool enough to handle. Peel.

Using a kitchen towel, dry outsides of eggs and slice in half lengthwise. Put yolks in a medium bowl and set aside. Place whites in a resealable glass container.

Add the mayonnaise, coconut milk, mustard, 1½ tablespoons wing sauce, onion powder, and salt to the bowl of yolks. Using an immersion blender, whip until smooth. Spoon mixture into a large zip-top bag and snip a hole in a bottom corner.

Pipe mixture into egg whites and garnish with bacon, green onions, and remaining ½ tablespoon buffalo sauce before serving.

PREP AHEAD

Hard-boil and peel eggs

Cook bacon

Chop green onion

MAKE AHEAD

Refrigerate up to 8 days; leave bacon on side and add just before serving

---

NOTES AND SHORTCUTS

Sub smoked salmon for bacon

Sub dairy-free ranch dressing for buffalo wing sauce

Buffalo Wing sauce brands: Primal Kitchen and Noble Made

Add crumbled goat cheese or blue cheese for garnishing, if dairy is tolerated

Make-Ahead Sides

Broccoli-Crunch Salad

SERVES 6
ACTIVE TIME: 12 MINUTES

¾ cup avocado oil mayonnaise

2½ tablespoons red wine vinegar

2 teaspoons date syrup

½ teaspoon Healthy in a Hurry Burnt Broccoli Seasoning (optional; page 36)

Sea salt and black pepper

6 cups chopped broccoli, florets and stalks

½ cup chopped cooked sugar- and nitrate-free bacon

½ cup raisins

¼ cup chopped dry roasted cashews

¼ cup sprouted sunflower seeds

½ red onion, minced

In a large bowl, whisk together mayonnaise, vinegar, date syrup, and broccoli seasoning (if using), then season with salt and black pepper. Add chopped broccoli, bacon, raisins, cashews, sunflower seeds, and onion and mix together to coat with sauce.

Serve immediately.

PREP AHEAD

Whisk dressing ingredients

Chop broccoli florets

Refrigerate cooked bacon up to 4 days

Mince red onion

MAKE AHEAD

Refrigerate salad up to 8 days

NOTES AND SHORTCUTS

Use less vinegar if mayonnaise is more sour

Sub honey for date syrup

If omitting broccoli seasoning, add an additional pinch of salt and pepper

Coconut-Lime Cauli Rice

SERVES 4

ACTIVE TIME: 10 MINUTES

1 small head cauliflower, cut into florets

2 teaspoons coconut oil

¼ cup chopped fresh cilantro

¼ cup full-fat coconut milk

1 tablespoon fresh lime juice

2 teaspoons honey

¾ teaspoon sea salt

In a food processor fitted with a grating attachment or using a box grater, "rice" cauliflower. Pick out any large fragments that didn't get shredded and save for another use.

In a large skillet over medium heat, melt oil. Add cauliflower and sauté for 5 minutes. Add cilantro, coconut milk, lime juice, honey, and salt and cook for 15 minutes, until cauliflower is tender and liquid has been absorbed.

Serve immediately.

PREP AHEAD

Rice cauliflower and refrigerate up to 2 days

MAKE AHEAD

Refrigerate up to 5 days; reheat in dry pan, uncovered, over medium-high heat for 3 to 5 minutes

Freeze up to 3 months; reheat in dry pan, uncovered, over medium-high heat for 8 to 10 minutes

NOTES AND SHORTCUTS

Substitute 2 (12-ounce) packages frozen cauliflower rice for head of cauliflower

Ambrosia Fruit Salad

SERVES 6

ACTIVE TIME: 15 MINUTES

4 to 5 ounces plain, unsweetened dairy-free yogurt

2 tablespoons honey

2 teaspoons fresh lemon juice

1 teaspoon poppy seeds or chia seeds, plus more for sprinkling

½ teaspoon vanilla extract

8 cups mixed fresh fruit, such as kiwi rounds, halved green grapes, mandarin orange segments, sliced strawberries, diced pineapple, or blueberries

½ cup diced marshmallows

½ cup toasted unsweetened coconut flakes

In a large bowl, mix together yogurt, honey, lemon juice, poppy seeds, and vanilla. Add fruit and toss gently to coat. Stir in marshmallows and top with coconut flakes. Sprinkle a few more poppy seeds over top.

Serve cold.

PREP AHEAD

Slice fruit

Dice marshmallows

MAKE AHEAD

Refrigerate yogurt mixture up to 3 days

Refrigerate salad up to 5 days

NOTES AND SHORTCUTS

Sub precut fruit from produce section or thawed frozen fruit for fresh

For homemade honey-sweetened marshmallows, see daniellewalker .com/marshmallow

Curried Vegetables

SERVES 4 TO 6

ACTIVE TIME: 15 MINUTES

2 teaspoons coconut oil	Zest of 1 lime
4 cups broccoli florets	1 tablespoon coconut aminos
1 cup shredded carrots	1 teaspoon ground cumin
1 cup sliced zucchini	1 teaspoon ground turmeric
8 ounces sugar snap peas	½ teaspoon ground coriander
2 garlic cloves, minced	¼ teaspoon ground nutmeg
1 teaspoon grated fresh ginger	¼ teaspoon cayenne pepper
2 tablespoons fish sauce	1 cup full-fat coconut milk

In a large skillet over medium-high heat, melt coconut oil. Add broccoli, carrots, zucchini, snap peas, garlic, and ginger and sauté for 4 to 6 minutes, until vegetables are crisp and bright. Add fish sauce, lime zest, coconut aminos, cumin, turmeric, coriander, nutmeg, and cayenne and let simmer for 3 to 5 minutes, until vegetables are cooked but still firm. Pour in coconut milk, cover, and steam for 5 minutes.

Serve hot.

PREP AHEAD

Cut broccoli florets

Shred carrots

Mince garlic

Grate ginger

MAKE AHEAD

Refrigerate up to 1 week

NOTES AND SHORTCUTS

Purchase pre-shredded carrots and cut broccoli florets

Sub 2 (16-ounce) packages frozen stir-fry vegetable mix for fresh vegetables

Sub 1 tablespoon curry powder for seasonings if you tolerate nightshades

Sub 1 teaspoon sea salt for fish sauce

Roasted Pineapple and Sweet Potatoes with Cinnamon-Cashew Drizzle

SERVES 4 TO 6
ACTIVE TIME: 40 MINUTES

1 pound garnet sweet potatoes, scrubbed clean and cut into 1-inch cubes

1 small pineapple, cored, peeled, and cut into 1-inch cubes

3 tablespoons melted coconut oil

½ teaspoon ground cinnamon

¼ teaspoon sea salt

¼ teaspoon chili powder

⅛ teaspoon ground coriander

¼ cup unsweetened raw cashew butter

1 tablespoon melted ghee

2 teaspoons pure maple syrup

Fill a large pot with water and bring to a boil. Add sweet potatoes and blanch for 2 minutes, then remove and drain immediately in a colander. Place potatoes on a kitchen towel to dry.

Preheat oven to 425°F. Line a half sheet pan with parchment paper.

Place pineapple and blanched sweet potatoes on prepared pan and toss with oil, ¼ teaspoon cinnamon, salt, chili powder, and coriander. Roast in oven for 15 minutes. Toss and return to oven for 15 minutes longer. Turn oven temperature to broil and cook for 2 minutes, until sweet potatoes are browned.

In a small bowl, whisk together cashew butter, ghee, remaining ¼ teaspoon cinnamon, and maple syrup. Drizzle 2 tablespoons sauce over roasted sweet potatoes and pineapple.

Serve hot, with remaining drizzle alongside.

PREP AHEAD

Blanch and cool potatoes

Peel, core, chop pineapple

Whisk drizzle

MAKE AHEAD

Refrigerate, drizzle stored separately, up to 1 week

NOTES AND SHORTCUTS

Sub butternut squash for sweet potatoes

Sub honey for maple syrup

Sub coconut oil for ghee

Instant Pot Mashed Potatoes

SERVES 4 TO 6

ACTIVE TIME: 30 MINUTES

5 pounds Yukon gold potatoes, peeled and halved if large

1 cup unsalted chicken bone broth

2 teaspoons sea salt

½ cup unsweetened cashew milk

⅓ cup full-fat coconut milk

½ cup ghee

Instant Pot: In an Instant Pot, combine potatoes, broth, and 1 teaspoon salt. Secure lid and set valve to seal. Cook on high pressure with a 6-minute timer. Quick-release pressure.

Remove inner pot and set on a towel. Using a potato masher or electric handheld mixer, mash potatoes directly in pot. Return interior pot to machine and set machine to sauté on high. Stir in ghee and cook until heated through. Turn off machine and season with remaining 1 teaspoon salt.

Stovetop: Fill a large pot with cold water and add potatoes and 1 teaspoon salt. Bring to a boil, partially cover, and cook for 15 to 17 minutes, or until fork-tender. Drain and return potatoes to pot. Add cashew milk, coconut milk, broth, ghee, and remaining 1 teaspoon salt and mash directly in pot.

Serve hot.

MAKE AHEAD

Refrigerate up to 1 week

Freeze up to 4 months

NOTES AND SHORTCUTS

You can sub russet potatoes or sweet potatoes, but I find Yukon gold to have superb texture when pressure-cooked

Sub 1 cup plain unsweetened dairy-free creamer, such as Nutpods, for cashew and coconut milk

Sub unsalted butter or Miyoko's dairy-free butter for ghee

Make-Ahead Desserts

No-Cook Banana Pudding Parfaits

SERVES 6
ACTIVE TIME: 10 MINUTES

1 (13.5-ounce) can full-fat coconut milk

½ cup hot cashew milk

⅓ cup white chia seeds

3 tablespoons light-colored raw honey

1 tablespoon melted coconut oil

2 teaspoons vanilla extract

¼ teaspoon sea salt

2 bananas, sliced

8 grain-free crispy cookies, crushed

In a blender, combine coconut milk, cashew milk, chia seeds, honey, coconut oil, vanilla, and salt and blend until a completely smooth pudding forms, about 45 seconds.

Add a few banana slices each to the bottom of 6 pint jars. Divide pudding evenly among jars, pouring it over bananas. Top pudding with remaining banana slices. Cover and refrigerate for 6 hours.

When ready to serve, add crushed cookies to tops of puddings.

MAKE AHEAD

Refrigerate up to 1 week; add cookies and bananas just before serving

Freeze up to 6 months

NOTES AND SHORTCUTS

Sub any dairy-free milk for cashew milk

Siete Mexican shortbread cookies, Hu snickerdoodles, or Simple Mills sweet thins work great in this

Cinnamon Coffee Cake

SERVES 8
ACTIVE TIME: 35 MINUTES

1 (11.5-ounce / 325g) box grain-free vanilla cake mix

2 eggs, at room temperature

⅓ cup (80g) plain Greek-style dairy-free yogurt, plus 2 teaspoons

¼ cup (60ml) dairy-free milk

3 tablespoons avocado oil

1 tablespoon vanilla extract

3 tablespoons maple sugar

2 tablespoons ground cinnamon

Preheat oven to 325°F. Lightly grease a 5 by 8-inch loaf pan.

Reserve ¼ cup (35g) cake mix.

In a blender, combine eggs, ⅓ cup (80g) yogurt, milk, oil, vanilla, and remaining cake mix and blend on low speed for 15 seconds, then turn speed to high for 30 seconds to form a batter.

In a small bowl, combine reserved ¼ cup (35g) cake mix, remaining 2 teaspoons yogurt, maple sugar, and cinnamon and stir to form a paste.

Pour half of cake batter into prepared loaf pan, spreading it evenly. In small spoonfuls, drop about one-third of cinnamon paste on top of batter. Using a knife or toothpick, gently swirl into batter. Pour remaining cake batter over cinnamon swirl, spreading it evenly. Add another one-third cinnamon paste on top and swirl gently into batter. Crumble remaining one-third cinnamon paste evenly on top.

Bake for 30 to 32 minutes, until a toothpick inserted into center of cake comes out clean. Transfer to a wire rack and let cool completely before serving.

MAKE AHEAD

Refrigerate up to 10 days

Freeze individual slices up to 6 months

NOTES AND SHORTCUTS

I prefer to use cashew milk for its richness

Sub coconut sugar for maple sugar

Any grain-free cake mix or even pancake mix will work here, but I prefer making my own to save money and control ingredients. Simple Mills or Bob's Red Mill grain-free cake mixes work best for store bought; be sure to use one that has sweetener and leavener (baking soda or baking powder), since it is not included in these recipes.

Scan QR code to sub a homemade flour mix (with a nut-free option) for store-bought cake mix

Balsamic-Basil-Strawberry Cake with Cream Cheese Frosting

SERVES 8
ACTIVE TIME: 35 MINUTES

CAKE

⅓ cup (80ml) unsweetened almond milk

3 eggs

1 (11.5-ounce / 325g) box grain-free vanilla cake mix

2 tablespoons melted ghee

2 tablespoons light-colored raw honey

2 teaspoons fresh lemon juice

2 teaspoons vanilla extract

MACERATED STRAWBERRIES

2 pints strawberries, hulled

¼ cup coconut sugar

2 teaspoons balsamic vinegar

FROSTING

6 tablespoons dairy-free cream cheese

¼ cup light-colored raw honey

2 tablespoons palm shortening

½ teaspoon vanilla extract

¼ cup fresh basil, thinly sliced into ribbons

MAKE AHEAD

Refrigerate frosted cake, berries separately, up to 1 week

Freeze individual cake slices up to 6 months; defrost at room temperature or overnight in fridge

---

NOTES AND SHORTCUTS

Sub fresh peaches for strawberries

Sub avocado oil for ghee

Use Green Valley or Good Culture for lactose-free cream cheese, Miyoko's for dairy-free

Sub coconut oil for palm shortening

Any grain-free cake mix or even pancake mix will work here, but I prefer Simple Mills; be sure to use one that has sweetener and leavener (baking soda or baking powder), since it is not included in recipe

Scan QR code to sub a homemade flour mix recipe (with a nut-free option) for store-bought

Save some macerated strawberries to serve with yogurt with granola; it's my favorite!

Preheat oven to 350°F. Lightly grease an 8½ by 10-inch baking dish.

To make cake: In a blender, combine almond milk, eggs, cake mix, ghee, honey, lemon juice, and vanilla and blend on high speed for 30 to 45 seconds, stopping to scrape down sides if needed. Spoon batter into prepared baking dish. Bake for 20 to 25 minutes, until a toothpick inserted into center comes out clean and top is golden brown. Transfer to a wire rack and let cool completely.

To macerate strawberries: Cut strawberries in halves (or quarters if large). In a medium bowl, using a fork, gently crush 1 cup strawberries to release some juices. Add remaining berries, coconut sugar, and vinegar and mix together. Cover and set aside.

To make frosting: In a small bowl, combine cream cheese, honey, shortening, and vanilla. Using electric hand beaters, cream together on high speed until smooth. Refrigerate to set.

Once cake is cool, cover with frosting and arrange berries and basil on top before serving.

Crustless Pumpkin Pies

SERVES 6
ACTIVE TIME: 5 MINUTES

2 (15-ounce) cans pumpkin puree

1 cup full-fat coconut milk

¾ cup pure maple syrup

6 eggs

1 tablespoon pumpkin pie spice

Zest of 1 lemon

2 teaspoons vanilla extract

1 pinch sea salt

Dairy-free whipped cream for serving (optional)

Preheat oven to 350°F.

In a medium bowl, whisk together pumpkin puree, coconut milk, maple syrup, eggs, pumpkin pie spice, lemon zest, vanilla, and salt until smooth and no lumps are visible. Equally pour into six 4-ounce ramekins and place on a baking sheet.

Bake for 25 to 30 minutes. Custards should jiggle slightly in center when removed from oven. Let cool to room temperature, then refrigerate for 1 hour.

Serve with whipped cream, if desired.

PREP AHEAD

Refrigerate unbaked pies up to 2 days

MAKE AHEAD

Refrigerate baked pies up to 10 days

Freeze baked pies up to 3 months

NOTES AND SHORTCUTS

Pumpkin pie spice is a store-bought mix of cinnamon, ginger, nutmeg, cloves, and sometimes cardamom

If using freshly roasted pumpkin, allow it to drain in a fine-mesh sieve before using

Sub honey for maple syrup

Sub 1¼ cups aquafaba, whipped until soft peaks form, for eggs

MAKE-AHEAD MUG CAKES

MAKES 4 INDIVIDUAL CAKES
ACTIVE TIME: 5 MINUTES

Lemon Poppy Seed

4 eggs

1½ tablespoons honey

Zest and juice of 1 lemon

2½ tablespoons avocado oil

2 teaspoons vanilla extract

1⅓ cups (197g) grain-free
vanilla cake mix

Vanilla Glaze (recipe follows)

1 teaspoon poppy seeds
for topping

Chocolate Birthday Cake

4 eggs

¼ cup water

1½ tablespoons pure
maple syrup

2½ tablespoons avocado oil

1⅓ cups (197g) grain-free
chocolate cake mix

¼ cup dark chocolate chips

Vanilla Glaze (recipe follows)

1 tablespoon dye-free
sprinkles for topping

Carrot Cake

4 eggs

1½ tablespoons pure
maple syrup

2½ tablespoons avocado oil

2 teaspoons vanilla extract

Juice of 1 lemon

2 teaspoons pumpkin pie spice

⅓ cup grated carrots

¼ cup unsweetened
shredded coconut

¼ cup raisins

1⅓ cups (197g) grain-free
vanilla cake mix

Cream Cheese Frosting
(recipe follows)

1 tablespoon chopped pecans
for topping

MAKE AHEAD

Freeze cake batter 6 months

Refrigerate all frostings and glazes
1 month

NOTES AND SHORTCUTS

Store-bought shortcut glaze: Melt
1 tablespoon Miss Jones or Simple
Mills dairy-free frosting per serving
and drizzle over top

Any grain-free cake mix or pancake
mix will work here, but I make my
own to save money and control the
ingredients. Simple Mills or Bob's
Red Mill grain-free cake mixes work
best; use one that has sweetener
and leavener (baking soda or baking
powder) because it is not included in
these recipes.

Scan QR code to sub a homemade
flour mix (with a nut-free option)

Sub coconut oil or unsalted butter
for palm shortening in frostings

Sub avocado oil or coconut oil for
ghee in Caramel Apple Mug Cake

CONTINUED

Caramel Apple

2 tablespoons coconut sugar

2½ tablespoons ghee

1 cup diced apples

4 eggs

2 teaspoons vanilla extract

2 teaspoons ground cinnamon, plus more for dusting

½ teaspoon ground allspice

1⅓ cups (197g) grain-free vanilla cake mix

Cashew Butter Glaze (recipe follows)

Place a 4-cavity jumbo silicone muffin mold on a small, rimmed baking sheet.

For each flavor, in a large bowl, whisk together all ingredients except the frosting or glaze and toppings (sprinkles, poppy seeds, pecans). Using a ladle, divide the batter evenly between the cavities, filling each completely. Cover well and freeze until solid, at least 12 hours. Pop the frozen batters out of the mold and store in an airtight container in the freezer.

To bake a single-serving cake: Place a frozen batter puck into a 16-ounce microwave-safe mug or ovenproof ramekin. Microwave on high for 2½ minutes until a toothpick inserted into the center comes out clean. Alternatively, bake at 350°F for 20 to 22 minutes.

Drizzle or spread 1 to 2 tablespoons of frosting or glaze atop the mug cake. Sprinkle with topping and serve.

VANILLA GLAZE

In a bowl, combine 2 tablespoons palm shortening (melted), 2 tablespoons honey, 1½ teaspoons coconut oil (melted), and ½ teaspoon vanilla extract and mix until smooth.

CREAM CHEESE FROSTING

In a bowl, combine 3 tablespoons dairy-free cream cheese, 2 tablespoons honey, 1 tablespoon room-temperature palm shortening, and ¼ teaspoon vanilla extract and mix until smooth.

CASHEW BUTTER GLAZE

In a bowl, combine 2 tablespoons unsweetened cashew butter, 2 teaspoons melted coconut oil, 2 tablespoons pure maple syrup or honey and mix until smooth.

Mint Pots de Crème

SERVES 6

ACTIVE TIME: 60 MINUTES (PLUS 3 HOURS' CHILLING)

1½ cups cashew milk

½ cup coconut cream

6 ounces dark chocolate chips or chopped bar

4 egg yolks

1 teaspoon peppermint extract

1 tablespoon maple sugar

Preheat oven to 300°F.

In a small saucepan over medium-high heat, combine cashew milk and coconut cream and cook until nearly boiling. Then remove from heat and stir in chocolate until melted and mixture is smooth.

In a large bowl, combine egg yolks, peppermint extract, and maple sugar. Whisking constantly, slowly pour hot chocolate into yolks. Strain through a fine-mesh sieve into a large measuring cup or bowl. Divide mixture among six 4-ounce ramekins or espresso cups.

Position a large roasting pan on center rack of oven. Place filled ramekins in roasting pan and fill pan with enough hot tap water to come halfway up sides of ramekins. Cover pan with aluminum foil; use a fork to prick holes in foil.

Bake until edges are lightly set (lift foil to check) but center is still jiggly—it will set as it cools—35 to 40 minutes. Transfer ramekins to a wire rack to cool completely.

Refrigerate for about 3 hours before serving.

MAKE AHEAD

Refrigerate up to 2 weeks

Freeze up to 6 months

NOTES AND SHORTCUTS

I prefer cashew milk for its richness and neutral flavor, but you may sub full-fat coconut milk

Sub coconut sugar for maple sugar

Sub vanilla extract for peppermint extract

Banoffee Bites

MAKES 12 BITES
ACTIVE TIME: 15 MINUTES

1 ounce dark chocolate, melted, plus shaved dark chocolate for topping (optional)

4½ ounces crispy grain-free cookies

¾ tablespoon coconut oil, melted

2 medium bananas, sliced ¼ inch thick

½ cup coconut sugar

¼ cup coconut cream

3 tablespoons raw cashew butter

2 teaspoons vanilla extract

Pinch of flaky sea salt for topping (optional)

In a food processor or blender, combine melted chocolate, cookies, and coconut oil and process until it resembles fine sand.

Press this mixture into bottoms of sixteen mini muffin cups, about one-fourth full. Place three slices of banana on top of each cavity. Place pan in freezer for 30 minutes.

Meanwhile, in a small saucepan over medium-high heat, combine coconut sugar and coconut cream, stir to incorporate, and bring to a boil. Turn heat to low and let simmer, stirring frequently, for 15 minutes, until deep amber and thickened. Remove from heat and stir in cashew butter and vanilla. Equally divide this caramel among muffin cups, filling to top.

Place pan in freezer for 2 hours. Once firm, transfer bites to an airtight container and store in refrigerator. Eat straight from refrigerator or warm slightly to enjoy. Top with chocolate shavings or flaky sea salt, if desired.

PREP AHEAD

Slice and freeze bananas

MAKE AHEAD

Refrigerate up to 2 months

Freeze up to 6 months

NOTES AND SHORTCUTS

Both Siete Mexican Shortbread cookies and Hu snickerdoodles work great in this

Make six bites in a 12-cup muffin pan, lined with parchment paper liners, in place of mini muffin pan

Gratitude

To this community of home cooks, your passion and creativity inspire me every day. I hope this book becomes an essential tool in your kitchen, relieving your mental load, reducing dinnertime stress, and easing decision fatigue. Thank you for being my motivation.

To my family, Ryan and my three beautiful kids, you have been my unwavering support throughout this culinary journey. To our extended family and friends, your help with childcare and dishes—and the "challenging" task of taste testing—has been invaluable.

To Paige Arnett, we accomplished this feat in record time, and I owe it all to your unwavering support in the kitchen, at the grocery store, and tackling the mountain of dishes in the sink.

To Kari Stuart, you're not just an agent but a true friend, a trusted sounding board, and a fierce advocate. Your presence in my life is a gift, and I'm incredibly thankful for you.

To Aubrie Pick, whose remarkable talent formed the exquisite groundwork for *Eat What You Love* and *Healthy in a Hurry*. I am grateful for the enduring imprint of your legacy in my books. I'll cherish each page turned, reminiscing about every shot, the laughter on set, and the shared energy. You were an extraordinary creative collaborator, and it pains me that we won't create together again. Aubrie, your absence is deeply felt, and I miss you profoundly.

To the photography and design teams: Lillian Kang, Paige Arnett, Erin Scott, and Emma Campion. Your talent and dedication brought this cookbook to life, making it both functional and beautiful for kitchens everywhere. Thank you for stepping in at the last minute and for turning these recipes and meal plans into works of art.

To Julie Bennett, thank you for embracing my vision, patiently accepting this manuscript in phases, and skillfully trimming my words where necessary. Your contribution ensured this book's usability for readers.

To my DW team, you are the backbone of all things: blog, emails, online cooking courses, social media, and beyond. Your hard work allows us to create and offer free resources, recipes, and content to our readers, while I'm head down creating and writing these books. We couldn't do it without you.

Recipe Index

Chicken

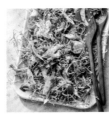

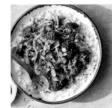

Green Goddess Grilled Chicken with Feta and Cilantro 194

Greek Lemon-Chicken Soup 197

Green Goddess Cobb Salad with Crispy Chicken Skin Croutons 201

Chicken Tinga 206

Chicken Souvlaki Lettuce Wraps 209

Taco Skillet Hash 210

Sheet-Pan Smashed-Potato Nachos 222

Baked Pesto Gnocchi and Sausage 245

Four Quick-Grilled Chicken Marinades 247

Beef and Lamb

Make-Ahead Beef and Lamb Meatballs 34

Cajun Steak and Cheesy Almond Grits 51

Stuffed-Pepper Soup 75

Enchilada-Stuffed Sweet Potatoes 96

Korean-Inspired BBQ Beef Bowls 130

Lamb Keftedes with Spicy Marinara 134

Granny's Spaghetti with Meat Sauce 144

Cheats Minestrone 146

Italian Cottage Pie 149

Prep Recipe: Shredded Beef 156

Beef and Zucchini Enchiladas Verdes 163

Steak and Eggs Breakfast Tacos 164

Magic Meatball Pasta 189

Cuban-Inspired Picadillo with Crispy Plantain Tostones 198

Thai Steak Lettuce
Cups 213

Tex-Mex Mac and
Cheese 224

Seafood

Spanish Rice with
Chorizo, Artichokes, and
Lemon–Garlic Aioli 56

Crispy Green Goddess
Salmon with Broccolini,
Potatoes, and Arugula 83

Cali Salmon Bowls 99

Citrus Salmon with
Orange-Cucumber
Salad 111

Roasted Halibut with
Potatoes and Lemon-
Olive Salsa 133

Fridge Clean-Out Veggie
and Shrimp Meal-Prep
Bowls 137

Smoked Salmon with
Roasted Asparagus and
Lemon-Caper Yogurt 159

Coconut-Curry Shrimp
and Sweet Potatoes 170

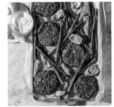

Salmon Cakes and
Roasted Artichokes and
Asparagus 174

Shrimp and Spaghetti
Squash with Feta-Tomato
Sauce 221

Cajun Salmon with Mango-
Pineapple Salsa and Coconut-
Lime Cauli Rice 227

Creamy Dill-Sardine Salad
with Capers 232

Mediterranean Salmon
Salad 234

Tuna Casserole 236

Tuna Salad with Apples
and Pumpkin Seeds 238

Lemony Shrimp Pasta
with Artichokes 239

Pork

Creamy Sausage and
Potato Soup 60

Egg Roll Bowls 84

Sausage and Fennel
Linguine 95

Prep Recipe: Shredded
Carnitas Pork 104

Fried Pineapple and Pork Rice 107

Cuban Pork Sheet-Pan Quesadillas 108

Smashed Potatoes and Chorizo with Jammy Eggs 125

Tomato Soup and Grilled Prosciutto-and-Pear Cheese Sandwiches 235

Breakfast-for-Dinner: Sheet-Pan Pancakes and Bacon 237

Sausage Skillets, Four Ways 240

Meatless

No-Boil Baked Pesto and Vegetable Penne 118

Pizza Night 122

Cheesy Broccoli Soup 160

Cream of Mushroom Soup 173

Coconut-Pumpkin Curry 233

Spiced Sweet Potato Soup 244

Make-Ahead Breakfasts

Blueberry Muffins 250

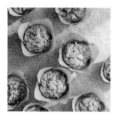

Savory Sausage–Chive Breakfast Muffins 251

Make-Ahead Poached Eggs and Instant Pot Soft-Boiled Eggs 253

Golden Chia Parfaits with Tropical Fruit 254

Bacon and Hash Brown Tray Bake 255

Bacon-Spinach Sandwiches 257

Make-Ahead Snacks

Prep Recipe: Cheesy Nacho Sauce 218

Coconut-Chocolate Hunks 260

French Onion Dip 261

Smoked Salmon Dip 262

Ranch Snack Mix 263

Cherry-Walnut Protein Cookies 264

Buffalo Bacon Deviled Eggs 265

Make-Ahead Sides

Prep Recipe: Mashed Roots 142

Broccoli-Crunch Salad 268

Coconut-Lime Cauli Rice 269

Ambrosia Fruit Salad 270

Curried Vegetables 271

Roasted Pineapple and Sweet Potatoes with Cinnamon-Cashew Drizzle 272

Instant Pot Mashed Potatoes 273

Make-Ahead Desserts

No-Cook Banana Pudding Parfaits 276

Cinnamon Coffee Cake 277

Balsamic-Basil-Strawberry Cake with Cream Cheese Frosting 279

Crustless Pumpkin Pies 280

Make-Ahead Mug Cakes 281

Mint Pots de Crème 284

Banoffee Bites 285

Index

Note: Page references in *italics* indicate photographs.

Meat. *See* Beef; Lamb; Pork
Meatball(s):
  Beef, 34
  Chicken, 34
  Chicken Parm, Skillet, 68, *69*
  Ginger, with Sesame Broccoli, *58*, 59
  Lamb, 34
  Lamb Keftedes with Spicy Marinara, 134, *135*
  Make-Ahead, 34
  Marsala with Mashed Roots, 150, *151*
  Pasta, Magic, *188*, 189
  Teriyaki, 48, *49*
  Turkey, 34
Mediterranean Seasoning, 37
Mint:
  Pots de Crème, 284, *284*
  Tzatziki, *208*, 209
Muffins:
  Blueberry, 250, *250*
  Sausage-Chive Breakfast, Savory, 251, *251*
Mug Cakes, Make-Ahead, 281-83, *282*
Mushroom(s):
  Meatballs Marsala with Mashed Roots, 150, *151*
  No-Boil Baked Pesto and Vegetable Penne, 118, *119*
  Soup, Cream of, *172*, 173

N
Nachos, Sheet-Pan Smashed-Potato, 222, *223*
Nacho Sauce, Cheesy, 218, *219*
Noodles. *See* Pasta and noodles
Nutritional yeast:
  Cheesy Almond Grits, *50*, 51
  Cheesy Broccoli Soup, 160, *161*
  Cheesy Nacho Sauce, 218, *219*
  Dairy-Free Parmesan Cheese, 33
Nuts. *See specific nuts*

O
Olive(s):
  Cuban-Inspired Picadillo with Crispy Plantain Tostones, 198, *199*
  -Lemon Salsa, *132*, 133
  Mediterranean Salmon Salad, 234, *234*

Onion(s):
  diced, storing, 15
  Dip, French, 261, *261*
Orange(s):
  -Cucumber Salad, Citrus Salmon with, *110*, 111
  -Sesame Chicken and Broccoli, 72-73, *73*
  Shredded Carnitas Pork, 104, *105*

P
Pancakes and Bacon, Breakfast-for-Dinner Sheet-Pan, 237 *237*
Parfaits:
  Golden Chia, with Tropical Fruit, 254, *254*
  No-Cook Banana Pudding, 276, *276*
Parsnips:
  Greek Lemon Chicken with Artichokes, *182*, 183
  Italian Cottage Pie, *148*, 149
  Mashed Roots, 142, *143*
  Meatballs Marsala with Mashed Roots, 150, *151*
  Roasted Tomato Italian Sausage Skillet, 243
  Sausage and Fennel Linguine, *94*, 95
Pasta and noodles:
  Baked Pesto Gnocchi and Sausage, 245, *245*
  Cheats Minestrone, 146, *147*
  Chicken Katsu with Mac Salad, 184, *185*
  Creamy Gnocchi Soup, 46-47, *47*
  Granny's Spaghetti with Meat Sauce, 144, *145*
  Lemony Shrimp Pasta with Artichokes, 239, *239*
  Magic Meatball Pasta, *188*, 189
  No-Boil Baked Pesto and Vegetable Penne, 118, *119*
  Tex-Mex Mac and Cheese, 224, *225*
  Tuna Casserole, 236, *236*
Pear-and-Prosciutto Cheese Sandwiches, Grilled, and Tomato Soup, 235, *235*
Peas:
  Citrus Salmon with Orange-Cucumber Salad, *110*, 111
  Curried Vegetables, 271, *271*

Ginger Meatballs with Sesame Broccoli, *58*, 59
Sweet and Spicy Chicken Stir-Fry, *86*, 87
Tuna Casserole, 236, *236*
Pepper(s):
  Cajun Steak and Cheesy Almond Grits, *50*, 51
  Herby Kale Salad with Ginger-Sesame Dressing, *62*, 63
  Mediterranean Salmon Salad, 234, *234*
  No-Boil Baked Pesto and Vegetable Penne, 118, *119*
  Sheet-Pan Chicken Fajitas, *176*, 177
  Shredded Carnitas Pork, 104, *105*
  sliced, storing, 15
  Spicy Cajun Sausage Skillet, 242
  Stuffed-, Soup, *74*, 75
  Teriyaki Meatballs, 48, *49*
Pesto:
  Dairy-Free, 32
  Feta, and Sun-Dried Tomato Sandwiches, *256*, 257
  Gnocchi and Sausage, Baked, 245, *245*
  Pizza Night, 122, *123*
  and Vegetable Penne, No-Boil, 118, *119*
Picadillo, Cuban-Inspired, with Crispy Plantain Tostones, 198, *199*
Pies, Crustless Pumpkin, 280, *280*
Pineapple:
  Korean-Inspired BBQ Beef Bowls, 130, *131*
  -Mango Salsa, 226, *227*
  and Pork Rice, Fried, *106*, 107
  and Sweet Potatoes, Roasted, with Cinnamon-Cashew Drizzle, 272, *272*
  Teriyaki Meatballs, 48, *49*
Pizza Night, 122, *123*
Poppy Seed Lemon Mug Cakes, 281, *282*
Pork. *See also* Bacon; Ham; Sausage(s)
  Cheats Minestrone, 146, *147*
  Egg Roll Bowls, 84, *85*
  Granny's Meat Sauce, 144, *145*
  Italian Cottage Pie, *148*, 149
  marinated, storing, 15

Published in the United States by Ten Speed Press, an imprint of the Crown
Publishing Group, a division of Penguin Random House LLC, New York.
TenSpeed.com

Ten Speed Press and the Ten Speed Press colophon are registered trademarks of
Penguin Random House LLC.

Typefaces: Bruno Mello's Binate, W Type Foundry's Joane,
and Johannes Erler's Carepack

Library of Congress Cataloging-in-Publication Data
Names: Walker, Danielle (Chef), author. Title: make it easy : a healthy meal prep and
menu planning guide / Danielle Walker. Identifiers: LCCN 2023057023 (print) | LCCN
2023057024 (ebook) | ISBN 9781984863096 (hardcover) | ISBN 9781984863102
(ebook) Subjects: LCSH: Comfort food. | Gluten-free diet—Recipes. | Wheat-free
diet—Recipes. | Quick and easy cooking. | LCGFT: Cookbooks. Classification: LCC
TX714 .W26158 2024 (print) | LCC TX714 (ebook) | DDC 641.5/639311—dc23/
eng/20240102
LC record available at https://lccn.loc.gov/2023057023
LC ebook record available at https://lccn.loc.gov/2023057024

Hardcover ISBN: 978-1-9848-6309-6
eBook ISBN: 978-1-9848-6310-2

Printed in China

Editor: Julie Bennett | Production editor: Patricia Shaw
Designer/Art director: Emma Campion | Production designer: Mari Gill
Production manager: Serena Sigona | Prepress color manager: Jane Chinn
Prop stylist: Erin Scott | Food stylist: Lillian Kang
Food stylist assistant: Paige Arnett | Photo and prop assistant: Brianna Kalajian
Lighting tech for location shoot: Brad Knilans
Retoucher: Lisa Iannarino
Copy editor: Dolores York | Proofreader: Robin Slutzky | Indexer: Elizabeth T. Parson
Publicist: Jina Stanfill | Marketer: Brianne Sperber

10 9 8 7 6 5 4 3 2 1

First Edition